C000093991

PRAISE FOR DAVE MACKAY

'The best player ever to pull on a Spurs shirt. If ever he was missing from the Tottenham side, every one of us had to work twice as hard to make up for it.'

— Jimmy Greaves

'Mackay was the man. He made everybody play. He made Spurs just as he made Derby later on. The fact that he achieved what he did in spite of two broken legs speaks for itself. What a man!'

— Denis Law

'Picking my ideal Scottish side takes a lot of consideration but I'd always start with Mackay, Captain.'

— Sir Alex Ferguson

'Simply, the best player I ever played with.'   — Jim Baxter

'When I look back on all the many and varied signings I made as a manager, Dave Mackay has to be the best. Not only did he have everything as a player he was the ideal skipper: a supreme example to everyone else at the club. He brought a swagger to the team and the whole of Derby County FC.'

— Brian Clough

'He was my best signing. He did more than anyone to forge a team capable of winning the Double.'

– Bill Nicholson

'The finest wing-half I ever played against.'

– Eusebio

'He was the one man I needed to help rebuild Manchester United after the Munich disaster, and had I got him it would have made the job so much easier.'

– Sir Matt Busby

'Any team that played Dave Mackay was basically cheating. It meant they had 13 players against your 11.'

– Alan Hudson

'We were just a good side until Dave Mackay came along. Then we became a great one.'

– Cliff Jones

'Quite simply and very sadly they do not make them like Dave Mackay anymore.'

– Johnny Haynes

THE REAL MACKAY

Dave and Isobel Mackay would like to dedicate this book to Thomas and Catherine Mackay, and Patrick and Ann Dixon. We could not have wished for better parents. Also to Johnny Harvey, Dave's mentor at Hearts. Without any one of these people, none of this would ever have happened.

Martin Knight would like to dedicate this book to Christopher Williams, who loved football, fishing and life.

THE REAL MACKAY
The Dave Mackay Story

DAVE MACKAY WITH
MARTIN KNIGHT

MAINSTREAM
PUBLISHING

EDINBURGH AND LONDON

First published in Great Britain in 2004 by
MAINSTREAM PUBLISHING COMPANY (EDINBURGH) LTD
7 Albany Street
Edinburgh EH1 3UG

ISBN 1 84018 840 5

'Charlie Tully'© Daniel McDonagh, 2003, reproduced courtesy of
www.footballpoets.org. 'Och Aye, Dave Mackay' published courtesy of
Ronald Macdonald

The author has been unable to trace the source of the newspaper article
entitled '£5,000 House and a Jag in the Garage' reproduced on pages
118–19. If an acknowledgement or an amendment to the text is required,
the publisher will be pleased to make any necessary arrangements at the
earliest opportunity

Every effort has been made to trace all copyright holders. The publishers
will be glad to make good any omissions brought to their attention.

A catalogue record for this book is available from the British Library

Typeset in Helvetica and Times
Printed and bound in Great Britain by
Antony Rowe Ltd, Chippenham, Wiltshire

Acknowledgements

I would like to thank the following, some of whom have assisted me with my recollections and all of whom have played a special part in my life and career:

All of the Mackay clan, especially Tommy, Frank and Ronnie
My wife Isobel, our children, David, Derek, Valerie and Julie, and our
  grandchildren Lisa, Daniel, Ria, Gregor, Lois and Lucy
John, Pat and Tom Dixon, and Ninian Cassidy
Des Anderson, Neil Martin, Jim Walker, Joe Kinnear, George Blues,
  George Armstrong and Frank Upton
Sidney Wale, Sam Longson, Ken Wheldon, Lionel Pickering and
  Mohammed Al-Mulla
Mr Hambly, Prince of Wales Hospital, Tottenham
Monty Fresco and Ken Jones
Les Gold and Dennis Webster
Tommy Docherty, Denis Law, Frank McLintock and Jim Baxter
Frank Cholorton, George McDonaugh and Alan Finley
Ian and Ann Gallagher of Gemini Windows and Conservatories, Derby

I am indebted to the diligence of Martin Knight and to all at Mainstream Publishing. A special thank you to Sir Alex Ferguson for providing the foreword for this publication.

I would like to express my appreciation to everyone whose name appears within this book and also for the generous tributes quoted.

I am immensely grateful to all my teammates from both my playing days and my time in management. I also wish to give credit to those who have inspired and encouraged me, in particular Mr Newlands and Mr Moyes from Saughton School in Edinburgh, Tommy Walker, Bill Nicholson, Brian Clough, Peter Taylor and Fred Ford.

Thanks also to many treasured friends from my days in Edinburgh, London, Derby, Nottingham, Kuwait, Dubai, Cairo and Qatar.

A final thank you for the enthusiasm of football supporters throughout my career; I hope you enjoy this trip down memory lane as much as I have.

Dave Mackay

Contents

Foreword

Everyone has their own vision of Dave Mackay etched into their memory box. A barrel-chested, square-jawed, buccaneering wing-half driving his team on with a shake of the fist is mine. However, when you are in his company, in the past or today, there is not a more placid man on this earth.

I played against Dave only once. I believe I was 16 years of age and trying to force my way into the first team at Queens Park. It was a reserve match and Dave was only playing because he was returning from a toe injury. He was by then an established player at Tynecastle. He was awesome and I knew I was privileged just to be on the same pitch as him. His aura and presence pervaded my whole intention of excelling and the radiance about him debilitated me on the night. Going in to tackle with Dave was like running full-on into a brick wall. We crumbled to a 5–0 thrashing.

After that, I followed his career with great interest and his excellent performance in the Scottish Cup final when Hearts beat Celtic 3–1 remains prominent in my mind. I knew when he went to England with Tottenham Hotspur he would scale new heights.

The better the footballers Dave played with, the better he got. He had two good feet, his passing was world class and he was a leader. I delighted in the incredible successes of the Tottenham side of the early 1960s and swooned at the romance of Dave reviving Derby County so spectacularly in the twilight of his playing career. The partnership between him and Brian Clough was a joy to behold.

It dawned on me when assessing his career that everywhere he went he was the mainstay of the team. He was the focal point of the team's energy, enthusiasm and will. I have always believed that football throws up a player for every era and Dave is *the* player of his era, representing strength, dignity, fairness and value for money. He played the game in the right manner, never complaining; he knew it was a man's game and conducted himself accordingly. Contrary to the myths and legends that have grown up around him, Dave was never dirty or cynical. He would never do anything that might sully the reputation of the sport he loved. He never set out to hurt another player, although plenty of others set out to hurt him, such was his influence over a side and their destiny.

The qualities of honesty, skill, leadership, industry and courage are perhaps rarer today, especially all rolled into one player, but I see Dave in Roy Keane and Steven Gerrard, and a little while back in Bryan Robson. I think that Dave sought those qualities in players when he became a manager. Archie Gemmill and Bruce Rioch spring to mind as footballers that excelled under Dave, and let us not forget the substantial success he enjoyed as a manager.

He was the best Scottish player in an era of excellent Scottish players yet he won only 22 caps. This was due to an inbuilt prejudice against so called 'Anglo-Scots' on behalf of the Scottish selectors. It is ridiculous but true that Dave and Denis Law paid the penalty for any poor performance on Scotland's part on a regular basis. Mackay could and should have captained Scotland for 15 years.

That famous picture of Dave Mackay manhandling a terrified Billy Bremner hangs in my office. Dave says he is not over-fond of the picture because he fears it portrays him as a bully. I disagree with that. Dave and Billy were fellow Scots and had played against each other many times. They both admired and liked each other. Dave's rage is that of a person having been inexplicably kicked by a brother or best friend; Billy's look is one of the brother or best friend having made a stupid mistake and regretting it.

Over the last decade, I have had the good fortune to get to know Dave well and value his advice and relish his company. He has not changed one bit and has retained that quality of humility that makes people great.

Sir Alex Ferguson, 2004

PART ONE

Hearts

CHAPTER ONE

The Real Mackays

I can't recall my first memory. I have a few, but it's hard to say categorically which one really came first. That has always annoyed me because I like to keep things in order. I like to think it was the day I slipped under the big iron entrance gates to Tynecastle, home of my local football club Heart of Midlothian, and stood absolutely alone on the empty terrace for a few breathtaking seconds. I remember swinging my little body under a crush barrier before leaping back down the steps, diving under the gate and running out onto Gorgie Road and back to our house in Glendevon Park. I suppose I must have been at school by then; I don't believe I would have strayed that far from the house if I was yet to reach five years of age. Yet I am clear that I literally rolled under the gate with space to spare between the concrete and the sharp edge of the gate. That chink of space could not have been more than a foot from the ground. A few years later, I would do it again, on a regular basis, to watch my Hearts heroes in action, but by then rolling under the gate was out of the question. I wriggled. When I reached my teens, I had to accept that I needed to pay but it was worth it because by that time the legendary Willie Bauld was playing. There had been nobody quite like 'King Willie' at Hearts and there has been nobody since.

I wouldn't have felt like an intruder or that I was doing anything very wrong when I stole into the ground. Hearts Football Club was as much a part of our local community as the golf club and park at the bottom of my road, or the prison and the school nearby, and you can't really intrude into a place that belongs to you and yours.

I was born at 18 Glendevon Park, Edinburgh, on 14 November 1934 and would live there until I found success as a professional footballer. I was named David Craig Mackay. The Craig came from my mother's maiden name. My grandchildren, I'm sure, would love it if the registrar had been sloppy and recorded me as Craig David Mackay. Dark clouds were gathering over Europe in the year of my birth. Winston Churchill was weary of standing up in the House of Commons and warning anyone that would listen about Herr Hitler and his rush to arms. He believed war was a real possibility and that Britain was in no position to defend itself against a Germany armed to the teeth. The problem was that nobody was listening. It would be five years before they did.

Not that any of this would have permeated down to me and my three brothers. Tommy was a year older than me, Frank a year younger and Ronnie came along just before the war actually broke out. We didn't have a television and if we owned a radio, we boys never listened to it. Even though Dad worked for the newspaper and would always bring one home with him, we rarely picked it up. From the time we could walk, our lives were out in the fresh air, in the road or under the bridge and into the park. That was our world. We were a tight-knit community – a phrase much-used these days, often to describe communities that are anything but. In our case, it was true, though. Everyone knew everyone else. We were all in the same boat and there was no question of keeping up with the McJoneses. Nobody's parents had a better car because nobody's parents had a car. Glendevon Park, on the outskirts of the city of Edinburgh, was working class, but I don't think it was particularly poor. I'm not sure what working class really means. We were a class of people who worked (when there was work, that is, and in the 1930s that was far from guaranteed), so I assume that makes us working class. But I have to report, I never encountered abject poverty. I knew of no kids that had to steal to eat, or of drunken or abusive parents, street gangs or prostitutes. Nobody bullied me. I was not scarred by any horrific early experience. Sometimes today, when I see or read about childhood memories, I think I must be the only person who had a happy and fulfilled early life. But I did. We all did.

Dad's printer's wages were enough to enable him to buy our home. Glendevon Park was a mixture of corporation and privately owned houses, although there was no way of telling the difference from the outside. It was not an issue. I don't know what Dad paid for our home, but I do remember half a century later when he called me and complained bitterly: 'Davie, I had a man today come to the house to quote me for a new front door. He told me that it would cost £750. Can you believe that? I told him to swing his hook. That's more than I had paid for the bloody house!' If I remember rightly, Dad collared the local painter and got him to splash on a coat of maroon paint instead.

I expect one of the reasons us boys were encouraged to play outside was that my dad, Tom, worked nights and slept during the day. He was a linotype operator on *The Scotsman* and he would leave the house at five every afternoon to take the bus to the Bridges in town where he did his bit to bring out Scotland's premier newspaper each morning. It was a good job – reasonably well paid and very secure in those more austere times. Due to his nocturnal hours, therefore, Mum was the one who had the task of keeping four growing boys in order. It was a task she rose to well, especially when Dad joined the RAF as war broke out in 1939 and she truly was doing the job single-handedly. The rules were clear. We stayed out either till 8 p.m. or whenever it got dark, whichever came first, and then we were all in bed by 9 p.m. It was a two-bedroom house and Mum and Dad had one room and all us boys the other. At around 5 p.m., she would stand at the front door and call us in for tea. She rarely had to shout twice, even if we were down the bottom of the road or in the park. If we did stray and

21

were late either for tea or 'coming-in' time, we knew we would get a clip around the ear. And she could punch, my mother. None of us ever resented this, either then or now. It was simple – if you didn't want a clump, you came in when she called. She was a small lady (4 ft 6 in. in her hobnail boots) and knew that, with Dad away, if she gave us an inch we'd take a mile. Millions of young mothers were in the same boat. How I wish she were here to give me a clump now.

If money got tighter, as it must have done with Dad no longer earning his printer's wage, we never noticed. We had warm clothes and good shoes, and there was always food on the table. What more could a boy need? And when Dad came home on leave, our eyes would be clamped on his haversack as we eagerly waited for him to open it up and pass us the little presents of sweets and chocolate that he would always bring back. But even then, when Dad was home, we still rushed our food down to get back outside and play with the other kids.

I don't think we ever played anything else other than football. Games were fluid affairs that lasted all afternoon and into the early evening. Players joined for an hour or so and then wandered off for tea or to go to the shop. Just before dark, they might be back for the last half-hour. Team numbers could reach 20-a-side and players would swap teams mid-game if the match was becoming too one-sided. It was not about winning. It was about enjoying ourselves and improving our skills. We all took a turn in goal so everyone could have their go out on the pitch. It was all very democratic and inclusive. Everyone wanted to be a forward. Nobody aspired to do anything other than score goals. Naturally, the goal-tallies reached ridiculous heights, although nobody was ever very sure of what the score actually was. When someone placed the ball between the posts, the more particular among our number would announce '23–19'.

'No way, it's 23–22,' another would protest. As if it mattered.

Even though our posts were of the lamp variety and our pitch a pot-holed and uneven tarmac, or a brown mud patch where the grass had been worn away through excessive use, these games honed our skills like no modern-day coaching school ever could.

It didn't matter to us that we would have to gather up the ball and stand back as the occasional Ford Popular came rattling down the street. By an early age, Tommy, Frank and I were good wee footballers – Ronnie was too young to play at that stage. Mind you, so was just about every other boy in the street. Wee footballer, by the way, was an apt description for me. I was 4 ft 6 in. tall and built like an anorexic jockey. I didn't start filling out until I got well into my teens. I never saw myself as a defender at first or sought the more physical side of the game. I fancied myself as a nippy outside-right or -left with the dribbling skills of Stanley Matthews and the shot of Hearts' own Alfie Conn. To this end, I would take our ball and go down alone to the railway bridge at the bottom of the road and practise. The wall of the bridge was particularly useful because it was made from stones that protruded outward and when you kicked the ball against it there was no way of telling at what angle it would come back to you. Maybe it was those countless hours of reacting to the wall and anticipating its rebounding direction that gave me my first instincts and grounding as a more defensive player. Bobby Baxter, my first Hearts hero, was a strong defender. He was also a miner at the nearby Gilmerton pit and turned out for Hearts on a Saturday literally an hour after coming up from the bowels of the earth in the cage. Perhaps then I did identify with the midfield and defensive players more than the average boy. Certainly, I was conscious of my lack of height and build, and tried to compensate for this by being combative and industrious on the field. I never shirked from a tackle, sometimes with boys twice my size, and ran for almost every ball. Even at ten years old, I could not stop myself harrying, encouraging and sometimes bollocking my teammates. I'm sure those who didn't take the game quite as seriously as me found it over the top and annoying.

In 1939, I started at Balgreen Primary School and would spend all six war years there. Whilst I knew Dad and most of the other kids' fathers were away fighting in the conflict, I don't recall ever being worried about the war or its possible outcomes. It was not a great topic of conversation amongst us kids and the grown-ups did a great job of keeping the reality of it all away from us. That would be impossible now. I think a couple of bombs dropped in Edinburgh, probably intended for the Forth Bridge, but ended up plopping down on old Edinburgh Zoo. The Germans may have frightened the odd giraffe but they did not scare us.

Everyone was football mad at Balgreen. After me, Gary Mackay (no relation) was another Balgreen pupil who would go on to reach the top in the Scottish game. (Later, and again after me, Graeme Souness would be a pupil at Saughton, my next school.) I can still remember the school song that we performed with gusto every morning in assembly:

> We are pupils of Balgreen School,
> Play the game has always been the rule,
> All day long midst the happy throng,
> The boys and girls of Balgreen School.

I was delighted when soon I was picked to play alongside my brother Tommy in the school team. There was a problem though: I did not possess a pair of football boots. Jim Hutton, a boy in my class, was growing much faster than I was and had quickly outgrown his old pair. He offered to sell them to me for seven shillings and sixpence. Although this only equates to 37½p today, it was no insignificant sum then. Looking back on it, I reckon Jim was having me over – I'm sure he couldn't have paid that for them new. Nevertheless, I asked Mum and she decided I could have my Christmas present early and handed me three half-crown savings stamps that I could exchange at the post office for 7/6d in cash. Good old Mum. I jumped onto the next bus into town and as I jauntily walked into the post office, I put my hand into my pocket for the stamps and experienced a feeling of horror in the pit of my stomach as I realised they were not there. They were with me when I boarded the bus; I knew that because I had felt in my pocket to ensure they were. They must have fallen out on the bus seat. The chances of recovering them were slight. What would I say to Mum? How could I lose her Christmas Club savings? They were the only things in my pocket besides a conker and a fluff-covered lemon bon-bon. They were not at the bus stop outside the post office and not on the bus taking me home (that would have been a miracle anyway as I was on a totally different vehicle), but as I alighted and crossed the road to where I boarded my first bus, there they were on the pavement. I could not believe it. I must have pulled them out of my pocket when I checked for them and they had fallen to the ground. No one had picked them up and the wind hadn't blown them away. I hurried back to the post office and neither Mum nor Jim Hutton, for that matter, were any the wiser. Jim Hutton loved his 7/6d and I loved the boots. Sadly, at my age, they do not get much wear these days.

By this time, my brother Tommy had taken a job – in fact he had taken two: a milk round in the morning and an evening paper round in the late afternoon. He was performing the role of eldest son in a family with an absent father well and I decided to join him. We earned ten shillings a week for this and handed it straight over to Mum who, one way or another, gave it straight back to the four of us. My motives for joining Tommy at the crack of dawn and then again at the fall of dusk were not completely altruistic. We took a tennis ball with us and played a game whereby he delivered to the houses on one side of the road and me to the other, and we had to keep the tennis ball in play whilst simultaneously shoving the *Evening News* through people's letter boxes. We did the same thing in the morning on the milk round, although this was more precarious. Both rounds were finished at a furious pace and only occasionally did we drop a pint of milk. Ernie may have been the fastest milkman in the west, but the Mackay brothers were the nippiest milkboys in Scotland.

I think it was in my second to last year that I careered into a boy in the year above me. During the lunchtime break, we played a chaotic game of football with a tennis ball. It had no rules, no goals and no real start or finish. One boy would start dribbling across the playground with the ball and then others would try to dispossess him of it. At its peak, there could be 50 or 100 boys in a pack charging backward and forward. Inevitably, boys sometimes got hurt in this hybrid of football, rugby and British Bulldogs. The boy in question was considered to be the third 'hardest' in his year. Yes, boys really do rank each other as such

at that age. Well, they did then. He came dashing towards me with
a posse of boys close on his heels and I nipped in front of him and
managed to put my foot on the battered tennis ball. Unfortunately,
he lurched forward over my whole body and fell to the ground.
Bad move. The game came to a halt and the air of anticipation was
high as the older boy brushed his trousers down and rose to his
feet.

'Sorry about that,' I pleaded earnestly.

'On the field, Mackay, after school,' he spat as he and his
entourage turned and headed back into the school building. I
looked at my brother Tommy, who was standing close by, and he
shrugged, giving me that 'what are *you* going to do now?' look.

Going back into class for the afternoon was torturous. In two
and a half short hours, I was expected to present myself on the
playing field to fight one of the toughest boys in the school. There
would be no teachers to break it up and I was sure to be bashed to
a pulp. I felt sick in my stomach and kept my hands under my
desk lest any of my classmates saw them trembling. It was an
awful couple of hours as I watched the hands on the clock on the
wall visibly pick up speed as they passed over the old, brown
roman numerals. I examined my options. I could go to a teacher.
I could run home. I could plead with the boy for mercy. There
were no options. Indeed, the more I thought about it, the more I
began to feel angry. After all, I had done nothing wrong. It was an
accident. Everyone could see that. I was younger and smaller with
no appetite for fighting, therefore the older boy was a bully and I
have never been able to abide bullies. There is nothing worse. As
the afternoon wore on, my fear subsided and was replaced by a
simmering anger.

At 3.30 p.m., I was shocked to see that a crowd of over half the
entire school was heading towards Saughton Park, opposite the
school, to witness the massacre. There is nothing like the scent of
blood to galvanise schoolboys. Well, there was no television for
them to rush home to then. A circle of bodies formed and my
opponent and I stepped into it. I rolled up my sleeves and adopted
a classic prize-fighting pose: legs apart, one arm outstretched and
the other guarding my chin. I'm sure I detected a flicker of

uncertainty on my challenger's face. I was by now determined to go down fighting and I advanced on him. Bang. Bang. I just kept stepping towards him. Bang, bang, bang. He stepped back and the human ring moved back to accommodate us. I continued to advance on him. If he returned a punch, I don't remember it. As the fluid boxing ring passed the tennis courts, the bigger boy went down. The fight was over. I was shocked because it couldn't have been easier and I was even more shocked because I thoroughly enjoyed myself.

I found out later that my older cousin Andrew Walker was in the throng and he told me that if I had started to take a hiding, he would have stepped in and sorted it out. Fortunately, that didn't happen; I think I would have been mortified if it had. That was my first real fight and, as far as I can recall, my last during my schooldays. The other chap never challenged me again nor did he ever speak to me. On the strength of about ten blows, I seemed to acquire a reputation – 'Davie Mackay, he's a tough wee laddie, he can box, you know', all that sort of thing – and the rough diamonds left me alone. I was happy about that. I had no truck with scrapping; all I wanted to do was play football. My dislike of bullies, though, has remained with me throughout my life and in my remaining years at Saughton, I intervened now and then when I saw someone being picked on.

Although I could not box and had no training or experience, there may well have been a pugilistic gene in the Mackay family that came through that day. Dad had played football for junior club Portobello Thistle in the late 1920s and had been a good player, but he and his brother Louis had both fought in the ring too. Dad even taught boxing at a school in his spare time. Years ago, it was not uncommon for men to take up the sport as well as football or rugby and, in the services especially, boxing was embraced by far more people than it is nowadays. All kinds of people became accomplished boxers; you didn't need to be big and burly or violently inclined. Norman Wisdom, for example, was an army boxing champion. Uncle Louis had a son, Louis (surprise, surprise), who was a couple of years younger than me and who followed his father's first-choice sport and really excelled, becoming a Scottish flyweight boxing champion in his own right during the 1950s and '60s. Looking back on it, living with Dad could be likened to Peter Sellers living with Cato. He liked to keep us on our toes and would often appear from behind doors or out of the pantry and start bobbing his head from side to side and shadow boxing.

'Keep your guard up, son,' he'd urge. In fact, I owe my trademark missing side tooth to one of these surprise attacks when he whipped his fist across the space in front of me and, unprepared as usual, I walked right into it. He was mortified, poor man. If ChildLine had existed then, I might have rung up. But then again, we didn't have a telephone.

At 11 years of age, I moved up to Saughton. Not the prison; the secondary school a mile and a half from our house. It was always a sore point, for the teachers at least, that they shared the name of the local jail, and a short while after I left, they changed the name to Carrickvale. Saughton was a big school and for the first time I came across boys from outside my immediate area – from being the oldest at Balgreen, I had the rude awakening of being among the youngest and smallest boys in the school. At first, I wondered if the school and prison staff job-shared – I found out to my cost that if you were late lining up in the playground before class, you received the strap. I, of all people, had no excuse for arriving late, as I was up and out of bed some hours before I was due at school, but somehow I managed it. One morning, my name was called out during assembly with a dozen other boys who were to attend the headmaster's study immediately after our uninterested rendition of 'All Things Bright and Beautiful'. Mr Denholm took us in one by one and I was told to extend my arm and open my palm. I clenched my eyes shut in anticipation of the swish of the strap that I had spied lying ominously on his desk. It hurt, but not enough to ensure I never visited the headmaster's study again.

The games masters at Saughton were a Mr Willie Moyes and a Mr George Newlands, and they encouraged me a great deal in my football. The game was their passion (I believe they were chiefly employed as technical and science masters, respectively). I think they were pleasantly surprised at our year's intake because a few very good footballers were developing fast under their guidance. The masters began to play me at left-half and it felt right. I had played at outside-left, left-back, inside-left – you name it – but now I had found my niche. Those positions sound so dated now, as I write. Wing-halves are from an age of Woodbine cigarettes, Old Mother Riley and cloth caps. I best stop there – I can feel the music from the Hovis ad coming on. Two other boys, Terry Tighe and John Paterson, joined me playing in the middle of the field and we struck up a great partnership. Terry was my best pal in and out of school, so we began to spend most of our time together. He and John were both football mad as well and we took our school team very seriously, although we were among the younger members. Jim Hutton, whose old boots I wore, was also in the side, as was my brother Tommy. By the time I became a teenager (not such a momentous landmark in a child's life as it was to become), the side had gelled and Tighe, Paterson and Mackay formed a fine-tuned defensive heart to the school team. We saw ourselves as a package and were all three delighted and excited when we were invited to trial for Edinburgh Under-15s.

The trials took place at Meggetland, not too far from our homes. Meggetland consisted of a series of pitches (only some of which had nets) with a small clubhouse at the centre. On the day, boys from all over Edinburgh gathered, but we were quite subdued considering the banter you would normally expect from a bunch of young male teenagers. Us boys were broken into teams and sent off to play one another on the pitches. You hoped for the goals with nets: first, because it is pleasing to see the ball hit the back of the net when scoring, and second, you don't have to run for miles to fetch the ball if there is a net to catch it. At the end of the short games, we were all assembled in the clubhouse and waited for the selectors to call out the final 11. These were the names of the boys that were chosen to play for Edinburgh Select, the city's Under-15 team. Everyone else would be surplus. Their trial would have been a failure.

The suspense was unbearable and I can't help thinking the selectors hammed it up a bit: 'Number one . . . goalkeeper . . . is . . . Peter Campbell' and so on. Most of us sat there and stared down at our feet. Praying. Terry and John's names were called and mine didn't follow immediately. My heart sank like a stone, but then I heard 'Mackay . . . outside-left'. I felt for the scores of boys whose names were not called and who were encouraged to gather their belongings and go home.

I played a few times for Edinburgh Under-15s, but my first performances were unremarkable. They were playing me out of position for a start (that was my story, anyway). Everyone was eager to impress and keen to display individual talents, and there was little team cohesiveness. During the matches in which I played, although I passed to whoever I thought was best positioned, very few of my teammates passed to me. Mum and Dad even came to watch and I felt that I had somehow let them down by not shining in these first matches. Never fear, though, because shortly after my 'breakthrough' in the Edinburgh Under-15s, I was to experience some real glory. My brother Tommy and I were about to make Mum and Dad the proudest parents in Edinburgh.

In my first couple of years at Saughton, Mr Moyes and Mr Newlands had not entered the team into the prestigious Scottish Schools Cup. There was some expense for the school, I guess, in travelling around the country to play other schools and they felt that the quality of the side did not warrant it. They knew the school had no chance and therefore did not enter us into the competition. However, after a successful 1947–48 season, in which Saughton scored 97 goals and conceded only 21, and we won 24 of our 25 league games, the school was entered for the Cup along with 127 other schools in 1949. I can't remember the path to the final, but before we knew it we had won our semi-final and were set to play Kings Park, a Glasgow school, at Hampden Park.

I could not believe that I was playing at Hampden at 14 years of age. Hampden: home of the Scottish international side; the stadium where Scottish heroes past and present had trod the turf. Hampden, where Tommy Walker, our man from Hearts, had shown the rest of Scotland what he could do. A crowd in excess of 10,000 was expected as supporters from Edinburgh and

Glasgow came to cheer on their schoolboys. The final attracted huge local interest and us boys were completely star-struck when the Hearts goalkeeper, Jimmy Brown, came to the school and announced he would be our coach for the final.

Unbelievably, the match ended in a 0–0 draw. I say unbelievably because when does a schoolboy match not produce goals? It was a hard-fought and exciting game, though, belying the scoreline, and there was nothing to choose between the two teams. We came off that pitch, all 22 of us, heroes, knowing we had given everything we could and produced an end-to-end entertaining feast of football. The crowd, which contained the extended families and neighbours of all the players, as well as the entire population of both schools, gave us the warmest ovation.

I was more delighted than most with the result because drawing meant that the replay would be at Tynecastle. Privately, I would rather this than even winning at Hampden. I would be playing on the Hearts pitch for the first time and I knew that we would win. I would not entertain the thought of any other outcome. Saughton High School closed for the day (much to the pleasure of even those pupils who had no interest in football) and all the boys, plus a good chunk of Edinburgh, set off for Tynecastle. It was another great game and I was so proud to run out on the pitch and hear the roars of appreciation from the 5,370 spectators that had paid to watch. It would have been a good deal more if it were not a weekday. This time we won 2–1 and the winning goal was scored by none other than Tom Mackay, who netted from a cross by yours truly. My chest still swells with pride when I think of Mum's and Dad's faces as they hugged Tom and me after the game. It was, up to that point, the best day of my life. It got better because after the game we marched down Gorgie Road and the two miles back to the school. A full bagpipe band led us, and people came out of their houses and applauded. Back on the school field, we tucked into orangeade and cakes as we basked in our new-found hero status. A few days later, I received my first review in the local paper: 'D. Mackay was the match's personality and helped immeasurably to weld the Saughton boys into a hard-hitting and solid defensive side.'

Something else happened that wonderful afternoon that I didn't find out about until a few years later. Had I known it earlier, I would possibly have died of pride and surely become an insufferable bighead. The great Willie Bauld, who not long before had burst into the Hearts first team after making his name at junior club Newtongrange Star, was at the match and at the end of the game had turned to Hearts trainer John Harvey and said, 'We'll no start winning anything until that wee laddie is playing for Hearts.'

CHAPTER TWO

Love Hearts

The match on that glorious day at Tynecastle crystalised everything for me. Up until then, I played football because I loved it and because that's what us kids did. I also loved Hearts, my local club, and dreamt that one day I might play for them. After collecting my medal against Kings Park, there were no mights. I was intent on becoming a Hearts player and determined to help the club become a great one. Hearts were the West Ham United of Scottish football: we always finished in the top half of the table and played attractive football, but never seriously challenged the Celtic and Rangers stranglehold on Scottish football – we wore maroon shirts, too. An ambition formed in my young mind to break through at Tynecastle and then lead them to glory. I was never one to be afflicted with self-doubt and didn't entertain the notion that this wouldn't happen. Little did manager Tommy Walker know that in Glendevon Park, a 14-year-old slip of a boy was hatching plans for his club.

Ironically, just as my old school has a connection with a prison, so too do Hearts Football Club. At the beginning of the nineteenth century, under the tower of St Giles' Cathedral in Edinburgh, stood the Tollbooth jail, also known as the 'Heart of Midlothian'. Although the prison was demolished in 1817, a dance club that flourished nearby in the 1870s was named after it. Local dancers who frequented the establishment decided to form a football team and started playing a mixture of football and rugby rules in the East Meadows area of town. Soon afterwards, Association Football rules were adopted and in 1875 this team of dancers joined the Scottish Football Association and competed in the Scottish Cup for the first time. In 1877–78, they defeated Hibernian to win the Edinburgh FA Cup and take their first honour. Incidentally, it took four matches to settle the tie and one of these was abandoned due to crowd trouble. Also, club captain Tom Purdie was attacked by a group of Hibs roughs when walking through Powburn Toll on his way home. Who said football hooliganism is a modern-day scourge?

In 1881, Hearts took over a site in Gorgie which became the first Tynecastle. In 1886, they moved again to the current site. The first match was a friendly against English side Bolton Wanderers and attracted a crowd of 5,500. In the same season, Hearts defeated Hibs in the Rosebery Charity Cup final, but again it took three attempts due to crowd trouble. The first match was stopped when enraged Hearts fans invaded the pitch because one of the players had his leg broken in a tackle with a Hibs player. In the second, the Hibs fans stopped the game when they went 2–0 down. And finally, in the third match, Police Inspector Mackay of the Edinburgh force marshalled a strong police presence to ensure the game could be played, and Willie Mackay scored the winning goal. You see, it takes a Mackay to sort out Hearts.

In 1895, Hearts won their first ever Scottish League Championship, pushing Celtic into second place and Rangers into third. The following year they beat Hibernian 3–1 at Logie Green (the only final ever to be played outside Glasgow) to win the Scottish Cup and the following season regained the Championship. This was truly Hearts' first golden age. In 1901, a forward called Bobby Walker was one of the scorers in a 4–3 Scottish Cup final win over Celtic. He was a Scottish international and was still talked about in reverential tones when I was a boy. Bobby played in the international match against England at Ibrox Park in 1902 when a part of the terracing collapsed killing 25 spectators and injuring 500 in what was to become known as the Ibrox disaster. When Bobby finally retired in 1913, the world-famous music-hall comedian and son of Edinburgh, Harry Lauder, organised a testimonial fund for him, such was his popularity.

When the First World War broke out in 1914, Hearts had opened the season with eight straight victories and looked poised to take the Championship for the first time since 1897. However, in November 1914, with a fierce battle raging in Ypres and the terrifying loss of British life, the entire first team, along with 400 shareholders and season-ticket holders, enlisted to defend their country. They signed up with 'McCrae's Battalion', Sir George McCrae's C Company section of the 16th Royal Scots. They were the first football club in Britain to do so and this cost them the Championship. With the squad seriously depleted, they fell at the last hurdle, yielding the title to Celtic. They had led the table for 35 weeks out of 37. Legend has it that many other clubs sheltered their players behind contracts and reserved occupations. Top goalscorer Tom Gracie, along with Duncan Currie, John Allan, James Speedie, James Boyd, Ernest Ellis, Henry Wattie and Alexander Slight Lyon – all of whom made the ultimate sacrifice – are now honoured by a memorial at Haymarket in Edinburgh and on the battlefield in France where they lost their lives. In the history of Hearts, the club's brave act of patriotism is considered by many to be their finest moment.

The players who returned from the Great War resumed their footballing careers, but many had been injured or gassed during the conflict and their abilities and strength were undoubtedly impaired. But the club and the fans were not of a mind to dispense with their services, such was the emotional bond between them and the city. The team were no longer a major force – indeed in 1922 they narrowly avoided relegation for the first time in their history. Players and trench survivors like Bob Mercer and Paddy Crossan never regained their full health and both died prematurely at the age of 37.

The club had a good year in 1932. A record 53,000 spectators were packed into Tynecastle to see Rangers defeat us 1–0 in the third round of the Scottish Cup. That was not so good, but a lad called Tommy Walker signed on as a junior that year as well. Not only would he serve the club as a great player (he became a top Scottish international and enjoyed a short but successful career in England with Chelsea), but he was also destined to become the most successful Hearts manager in history. He was an exemplary individual and professional footballer who had intended at one time to cut short his footballing career to work for the Church. The Second World War put paid to his plans with the ministry and cut into his footballing career. His early rise was meteoric. Courted by Arsenal but preferring to stay at Tynecastle, he was capped for Scotland as a teenager and famously scored the penalty against England in 1936 which made his side the first winners of the Home International Championship. In 1937–38, he spearheaded the team in a nail-biting campaign in which Hearts and Celtic swapped the table's top spot nearly all season. Celtic finally prevailed, but it had been Hearts' best League finish for many a year.

This is where I came in. Or under, so to speak. I don't remember exactly which game I first shimmied beneath the gate to watch, but it must have been in the early 1940s. I do remember being impressed by Bobby Baxter, Tommy Walker and Alex McCrae. The thrill of being packed in tight with all those other people, most of them strangers, cheering and shouting our boys on, stays with me. As does the wonderful leap of the heart when young Alfie Conn found the net and the general goodwill and banter as we all shuffled out of the ground and home after a victory. Going to the match was a ritual that really did bind the community together. For me, the only thing that beat playing football was watching Hearts.

I remember standing on the terrace at one of these first matches with Hearts trailing by two goals. Like others around me, I shuffled out of the ground despondent, almost tearful, having never before experienced a home defeat first-hand. There were still ten minutes or so left of the game, but I was crushed by the prospect of losing and seeing Hearts thoroughly outplayed. When I arrived home, my brother Tommy, who had heard the result on the radio, said, 'Great game!'

'Very funny,' I replied, downcast.

Hearts had actually won 3–2 and I had missed it all. I learnt then that a game is never over till it's over.

I can remember Tommy Walker moving down to Chelsea for a fee of £6,000 in 1946 and then bringing his new team up to Tynecastle for a friendly match. Although the Hearts faithful were heartbroken that Tommy had gone, there were no bad feelings and we knew that one day he would return. In that match, the famous England centre-forward Tommy Lawton was also playing. Although English football had only slightly more relevance to us than, say, Italian football, we all knew Lawton. He was a regular on the Pathé newsreels that were shown in our cinemas, along with Matthews, Mortensen, Mannion et al. We swapped cigarette cards with his image on the front. Chelsea trounced us 4–1 and, rather painfully, Tommy Walker bagged a hat-trick. Even so, he was still given an emotional standing ovation when he left the field. Mind you, most of us were already standing anyway.

Alfie Conn was already established in the first team. He was a smallish inside-right who possessed a stinging shot. Like others before him, but few after, he worked in the pit near his home in Prestonpans during his illustrious career. It is hard to believe that on a Saturday when he was out there poaching goals and covering every inch of the opponent's half, he had already worked an eight-hour shift underground. I can't imagine modern-day players arriving for work with the coal dust still embedded under their fingernails and ingrained along the frown lines of their foreheads. Come to think of it, I can't imagine Dave Mackay doing it. Alfie's boy, also named Alfie (didn't anyone in those days veer from naming the first son after the father?), carved out an even more famous career with Tottenham Hotspur and Scotland some 30 years later. But by then we had television to spread the word.

Conn Snr was good, but didn't become great until his two partners joined him in the first team. Jimmy Wardhaugh was first. True to Hearts' dancing heritage, he was nicknamed

'Twinkletoes' because of the way he glanced almost balletically past opponents and because of his amazing balance. His goal-scoring rate was amazing, too. By the time he was finished, he had managed 375 goals in 519 games and made a lot more for his two pals. The second, young Willie Bauld, joined Conn and Wardhaugh for his first-team debut on 9 October 1948. East Fife were the opponents that day and this attacking trio destroyed them by six goals to one, with Willie Bauld scoring three. The following week, Queen of the South were hammered 4–0 and Willie rampaged a hat-trick again. A buzz went around the ground, then Edinburgh, and finally Scotland. This was to be a very special partnership and Conn, Wardhaugh and Bauld were soon dubbed the 'Terrible Trio'. Down in England, the young Beverley Sisters breathed a sigh of relief.

Meanwhile, I was picked to represent Scotland as a schoolboy against Ireland at Kilmarnock's ground. I can't say I was capped because at the end of the match we were presented with a scarf and a tie. This was a godsend really because I spent the next few months wearing that scarf and tie everywhere I went, showing off. I would have looked even more of a berk than I clearly already did with a floppy old Scottish cap on my head as I strutted around my home town. We lost the game 3–2 and I didn't think I played well. The *Evening News,* however, said two other boys and I 'compared favourably against smarter Irish opponents'. Someone must have agreed because I was picked again, a while later, to play against England. And this one was at Wembley.

It had been an enormous thrill to play at Hampden Park, but even Scots had to admit that the pitch wasn't good and the lush green turf of Wembley took some beating. Also, there is no other ground in the world where a Scot wants to win more than at Wembley Stadium. There was great excitement in the Mackay household that I had been selected for the squad and that I would be visiting London and England. In my nearly 15 years on the planet, it would be my first trip across the border. I was the only boy from Saughton on the train down to Euston and, although the letter from the Scottish Football Association had told us that all our expenses would be covered, I sat quietly clutching the ten-shilling note Mum and Dad had given me for the trip. I was looking forward to seeing Big Ben, Tower Bridge, the gaslit streets where Jack the Ripper had once lurked, the River Thames, Highbury, St Paul's Cathedral, Buckingham Palace and the King's soldiers resplendent in red tunics and black bearskin hats. These were the images of London I had in my mind. Images I had gleaned from the cinema, from magazines such as *Picture Post* and from newspapers. Alas, I was to see none of this. We alighted at Euston station but were herded straight across the road to a grand and fine hotel. It may not in reality have been a grand and fine hotel, but I had never been to such a place before and things like chandeliers, bellboys, soft music and settees were enough to turn my head.

In the morning, a coach came to collect us and drive us out into the London suburbs and to Wembley Stadium. Before boarding, I had been up bright and early exploring the streets around the hotel and spending Mum and Dad's ten shillings on souvenirs and trinkets to take home to them. Sadly, I did not bump into any Beefeaters and my first impression of London underwhelmed me. The Euston, King's Cross and St Pancras area was not the most salubrious then, as now. However, the excitement and sense of occasion really built as our coach edged up Olympic Way and the famous twin towers came into view. A crowd of nearly 50,000 supporters was waiting inside and I was jealous as hell when the other boys donned their kits and ran out into the Wembley sunshine. I had been named a reserve, but was allowed to sit on the bench with the trainer and some other backroom staff.

We were under pressure from the start and by the near end of the first half, when the trainer pushed me onto the pitch, Scotland were lucky to be holding England at a goal apiece. I could see that England were outplaying and outrunning us, and in the second half, I felt what I saw. The English boys seemed so much bigger, stronger and faster. Their fitness was a level or three higher and it was embarrassing. Inevitably, the dam burst and England started to put the goals away like Steve Davis on a maximum break. One boy, whom I was trying to mark, controlled the entire rout. He held the ball in the middle of the field, deftly tapping it across to his teammates as I came hurtling towards him like an express train desperately trying to apply my brakes. He would then collect the ball again, as I lay prone, and pinpoint a forward in a good position and stroke the most stunningly accurate pass into his path. What a player he was! Barely 15 years old, but with the maturity of a full international. I was in awe, but aghast at the monkey he was making out of me. I was holding back the tears as we traipsed off the velvet grass having been hammered 8–2. I was already thinking about going home to Scotland having let my country down in such spectacular fashion. I was crushed and ashamed. I was also depressed, having brutally realised that there are levels in football and we were on a lowly rung compared with these English boys. One of my colleagues trotted up beside me and flung his arm around my shoulder. The result and performance had obviously not impacted on him in the same way. He wore a broad grin and whispered in my ear, 'Just think, it was only one each when you came on.'

I know it was a joke (not a bad one in hindsight) and in a perverse way he was trying to cheer me up, but that remark went through me like a knife. Did he have a point? Was it my inability to contain the boy genius that caused us to lose so dramatically? As I climbed the famous 39 steps to collect my loser's trophy from none other than the Prime Minister, Clement Atlee, I was in another world, having just accepted full personal responsibility for Scotland's ignominious defeat.

The journey home was a sombre affair. I read my souvenir programme and noted that one of the forwards that ripped open our defence was called Ray Parry. Ray was about to break through into the big time – shortly after that match, he became the youngest-ever player to debut for an English First Division side when he turned out for Bolton Wanderers at only 15 years of age. He went on to enjoy a good career with Bolton, Blackpool and England, and we were to cross paths many times. I was saddened to read of his death whilst writing this book.

The name on the teamsheet I really focused on was John Haynes, the captain. My torturer. He would become Johnny Haynes and, as I fully expected, a world-class footballer for

Fulham and England. Thank God I didn't know then that Johnny Haynes would have the opportunity to humiliate me again, only next time it would be on a bigger stage and in a different age altogether. That future ordeal would be filmed, televised, recorded for posterity and dragged out at every available opportunity to humiliate Scotsmen in every corner of the globe.

Back home, my parents and brothers did their best to snap me out of my black mood. I even considered packing in football and taking up some other playground sport. My temperament, though, was not suited to hopscotch. Dad gave me a bit of a talking to and told me that football, like life itself, is full of ups and downs and I should take it on the chin and not be so sensitive. He advised me that if I felt I was not good enough, I should make myself good enough and not just accept it. He also mentioned that he'd noticed I had made some bad tackles under pressure and had argued with referees. He told me to accept defeat graciously and never stoop as low as arguing with the officials, or deliberately or carelessly hurting another. They were principles I attempted to abide by all of my playing career and it may surprise you to know that I was never sent off in 30 years of competitive football.

Hearts Football Club pulled me out of the mire not too long after the Wembley debacle. I was invited along with some other Saughton boys to attend coaching schools at Tynecastle. Our Scottish Schools Cup triumph had not gone unnoticed, but I think they called me in for another reason. Matt Chalmers, the Tynecastle groundsman for many years, lived a few doors down in Glendevon Park and could not help but see all us boys constantly playing football, and he had kept an eye on us as we developed. He had recommended the club take a look at my brother Tommy and they duly signed him on – I believe he probably did the same with me.

Yet this was little more than them offering coaching and facilities to local boys – there was no commitment or contract of any sort. In exchange for the coaching, I suppose the deal was that if they spotted someone they really liked, they would keep them close and eventually offer them terms. I told people I was 'attached' to Hearts Football Club. It was still a great mark of status for me because it meant I changed in the same rooms as the Terrible Trio. I even saw them around the place, although I dared not strike up a conversation. Charlie Cox and Bobby Flavell, two other Hearts idols, gave us personal tuition and I felt I had arrived. One day, Bobby Flavell said to me, 'What do you want to do when you leave school, laddie?' I was a bit put out at this – it was obvious, wasn't it?

'I'm going to play for Hearts and Scotland, Mr Flavell,' I answered.

Bobby looked down at me and ruffled my hair.

'That's what I like to see,' he smiled, 'a boy with ambition.'

I was a bit disappointed he didn't say something like, 'I'm sure you will, son', but maybe he had heard about my Wembley game.

I adored school and it came as a rude shock when it sank in that I would really have to leave and enter the adult world. Where else can you get fed, see your pals every day, play loads of sports, have plenty of laughs and have absolutely no responsibilities? I well remember when Dad sat me down for a 'talk'. That sounded ominous. If I had known what they were, these 'talks', I might have suspected he was going to tell me about the 'facts of life'. Fortunately not.

'Well, son. It's time you decided what it is you'd like to do. Have you any idea?'

My blank expression said it all.

'How about we get you on the print with me?' I had guessed this was coming. Tommy had already joined Dad on *The Scotsman*. The print unions operated a closed shop and one of the perks was that jobs could be passed down from father to son, or, in Dad's case, sons. Although the trade unions in the print industry were strident and militant, I do not recall Dad striking or ever expressing unionist or particularly left-wing views. His philosophy was simple: a fair day's work for a fair day's pay. He never digressed from this. Indeed, his employers must have valued him highly because they persuaded him to work on beyond his 70th birthday when the normal retirement age is 65. This was also at a time when the industry was furiously shedding jobs wherever it could.

I didn't want to offend Dad, but I told him I did not want to take a job where I couldn't have Saturdays off to play football. In the print, they worked a shift system where this was not often possible. Dear Dad didn't point out that to get into the print was a rare opportunity, and it offered good wages and job security, while the football might not work out. 'OK, son, we'll have to think on this one then' was all he said.

Somehow Dad's brother Louis got me in as an apprentice joiner at the firm he worked for, Lawrence McIntosh Ltd. It was not the most obvious trade for me to enter as I had never shown an aptitude with my hands and had no interest in woodwork lessons at school. Beggars can't be choosers, though, and I couldn't think of any of the traditional trades where you had to be good with your feet. My duties included clearing up and working with the more experienced joiners when they went out on call to fit out shops or build shelves and cabinets for members of the public. Lawrence McIntosh himself was a hard man and a disciplinarian. He took an instant dislike to my habit of leaning on cabinets or up against walls.

'David Mackay, will you stand up straight. You make the place look untidy,' he would shout. He also told me off for moving around the shop floor noisily. I didn't really understand this: I was not speaking or whistling. He said clumsiness would be my downfall. How times have changed. If an employer barked at his employee to straighten his back nowadays, there would be uproar. But Mr McIntosh was a fair man, a product of his time, and not a bully. What he was telling me was for my own good. I think he knew deep down I would not make it as a joiner. My heart was in Hearts and, fortunately for me, so was his. Mr McIntosh was a huge fan of the club and about the only thing about me that impressed him was that I was 'attached' to it.

Groundsman Matt Chalmers was forever encouraging and pushing me in my football. He got me playing for Slateford Athletic, who, whilst still an Edinburgh juvenile side, were a step up from Saughton school football. I was still attending my coaching sessions at Hearts and was getting precious words of encouragement and acknowledgement from manager Davie McLean and assistant manager and local legend, the quietly spoken and kindly Tommy Walker. When Davie died prematurely,

Tommy slipped into his shoes. With Tommy in charge of the side and the Terrible Trio reaching their peak, there were just a few more pieces of the jigsaw to be added before Hearts would rise again. I did not know it then, but I was to be one of those pieces.

Terry Tighe and John Paterson had graduated from Saughton to Slateford with me and we were all very excited when junior side Newtongrange Star came in for us. 'Junior' in this context is a misnomer. Newtongrange Star were a leading semi-professional side in a league, perhaps equivalent to a Ryman or Isthmian league in England, and they were very senior. Most of the team was made up of men in their late 20s and 30s who had not quite cracked it as professionals or had played out short top-level careers and drifted downward. Us three boys were very much in the minority. The men welcomed us, though, and because of our youthful exuberance and enthusiasm, we did all the running and allowed them to focus mainly on their skills, which some of them possessed in abundance.

John, Tommy and I had done very well at Slateford Athletic, as had my brother Tommy and Eddie Kelly, who had also graduated to the side from Saughton. With the future Hearts goalkeeper, Willie Duff, between the sticks, we had won five trophies in two seasons. However, the move to Newtongrange was the biggest step-up yet and all of us learnt more in competitive matches from those older fellows in the Star team than in any structured coaching from the Hearts players and trainers. This is no criticism. We had gone live and there is no better education. At Slateford, we were basically the Saughton school side growing up together. Juveniles becoming men. At Star, or Nitten Star as the club was often called, we were suddenly amongst the men.

Star also had a real ground – Victoria Park – and a small but raucous set of supporters. These men and women were fanatical and, because we were dealing with smaller numbers, we got to know them and could recognise their faces and voices. They travelled away too, sometimes as many as a thousand of them, and did the locals know when they hit town. There was no hooliganism, but they could be wild and threatening, and I can remember games where the referee had to be held back afterwards for his own safety when decisions had gone against us. I dreaded losing or having a bad game in front of this lot.

One game is etched on my mind. It was against the charmingly named Ormiston Primrose and, other than what was about to happen, it was a fairly ordinary afternoon. Our inside-right was a lovely chap called Charlie Elms. He was one of the older men in the team I referred to, married and in his late 20s. To us boys, though, he was of a different generation and, although we did not socialise, he was always very kind, friendly and encouraging to us. I liked him a lot. He was a miner as well and maybe that day he had already put in a backbreaking, claustrophobic, ten-hour shift underground before turning out for Star. We'd been feeding balls through to him, but he didn't seem to be his usual alert self and shortly before half-time he passed me on the way to the dugout. 'I'll have to go off, son. I'm feeling groggy.' He walked off, but, and I am sure it is not just what happened next that has coloured my memory, he looked a shocking grey colour. It was a complexion I had never seen in a person before. I have seen it since, though.

At half-time, he was not in the changing-room and, as it was not my place, I did not ask where he was. I thought that maybe he felt so bad he may have taken the bus home. We played out the second half with ten men and when we came back into the changing-room, the manager and a few club officials and helpers were standing there.

'I have some bad news,' said one of the men, blinking back tears. 'Charlie died 15 minutes ago in hospital. It must have been his heart.'

I was dumbfounded and tears welled in my eyes. How could this be? I had been passing the ball to him only an hour earlier. He was just feeling a bit groggy. I had not experienced death yet. Only old people died in my book. Or soldiers. Or miners in pit disasters. Not fit, strong men playing football. As young lads engrossed in our own lives, we got over this tragedy reasonably quickly, but I still think of Charlie to this day and can only imagine the grief felt by his wife and family at the time.

One day, my boss Mr McIntosh announced that he was coming to watch me play for Star. I could not demur, as he had been fair to always allow me Saturdays off to play and further my football career. I expect he was checking that there was logic to his largesse. I thought I'd had a good game. By this time, all three of us – Paterson, Tighe and Mackay – were firmly established and some were saying we were the reason why the team was becoming a bit special.

'Can you take an honest opinion, Davie?' he enquired.

'Yes, Mr McIntosh, I can.'

'You will never make the grade.'

Fortunately, not everyone agreed with Lawrence McIntosh and the big clubs started to take an interest in us. Hibernian signed Eddie Kelly, the full-back who had captained the Saughton Cup-winning team for us, and they also signed Terry Tighe. I was a tad jealous but, shortly after Terry got his deal, Hibernian approached me and asked me to attend an interview with their famous manager Mr Hugh Shaw. I had mixed feelings about this. I wanted to play professionally more than anything else, but I was attached to Hearts in more ways than one. Hibs and Hearts are archenemies, always were and always will be, although their rivalry does not plumb the depths of the violent hatred felt between some Celtic and Rangers supporters. Or it didn't in my day. Nevertheless, it would be psychologically difficult for me to sign for Hibernian.

I poured my heart out to Dad and he listened patiently. His view was that if Hearts wanted me, they should sign me and that if they didn't, then I must go where I was wanted. Just the thought that Hearts might not want me broke my heart. Dad decided he was going for a walk. He never told me this and I never asked, but I do not think he walked very far. I believe he walked straight into Matt Chalmers' house, four doors down, and told him that his Davie was about to be offered terms with Hibernian and if Hearts wanted him they needed to act fast. The following day, I received a letter inviting me for a personal interview with Tommy Walker at Tynecastle. Funnily enough, it was scheduled for precisely half an hour before my interview with Mr Hugh Shaw.

CHAPTER THREE

Glory on Gorgie Road

Tommy Walker offered me £10 a week in the winter and £8 in the summer, bonuses for winning and a £20 signing-on fee. I couldn't have been better pleased. I was on a fiver a week with Lawrence McIntosh and the club were not expecting me to resign my job there. At least, not yet. This was good money for a boy barely 17. Very good money. Yet, I still told Tommy that I needed to discuss the matter with my family.

'Of course,' he smiled.

The upshot was that I agreed to sign, but said I would like to finish the season with Newtongrange Star first. I think Hearts were a little shocked that I hadn't bitten their hand off, but were relaxed that I was not going anywhere else. Still, they were not taking any chances – after the game against Armadale, Duncan McLure of Hearts walked home with me down Dalry Road. 'Are you ready to sign yet, David?'

'Yes, I think I am, Mr McLure.'

'That's grand,' he said, pulling a fountain pen and some forms from his inside jacket pocket. So, up against the crumbling wall of a tenement block, I signed for Hearts and fulfilled my first boyhood dream.

At home, this was a lovely period. For a short time at least, us three older boys were all attached to Hearts. Tommy had already signed and had been farmed out to Edinburgh City just as I had with Newtongrange Star, and shortly after my signing, younger brother Frank was also put on the books. Even Ronnie, the baby of the family, was following the family tradition by captaining his boys' team back at Saughton school. Guess what the main topic of conversation was in our house of an evening! The Mackay footballing family started to attract interest from the press and, more than once, young journalists arrived at our door for interviews and photographs. We were always on our best behaviour as we sipped tea with the reporters, dressed in our shirts, ties and woollen V-neck jumpers.

Whilst at Newtongrange Star, I was able to put right my disappointing junior international debut against Ireland. I was picked to play them again in 1951 and this time we prevailed by three goals to nil. Laurie Cumming, a respected writer on a variety of Scottish newspapers, had started to champion me in the press and he wrote:

> What a find Hearts have in 18-year-old [sic] left-half Davie Mackay. Top architect in Scotland's success, his grand positional play and strong tackling had the crowd voting him the best youngster they had ever seen in a junior national side.

At Tynecastle, I was now training with the first team and forced myself to have conversations with the likes of the Terrible Trio and my other Hearts heroes. I was still in such awe of these men and very much a shy boy who had yet to acquire adult social skills. Naturally, I became the victim of a typical new boy's joke. I didn't have much in the way of kit and, at one early training session, I was encouraged to put on a pair of plimsolls that were apparently going spare. This I did and joined in the five-a-side match being played on a concrete area. A few minutes later, Willie Bauld appeared and stood among us, hands on hips.

'Which one of you buggers has stolen my plimsolls?' he asked menacingly.

I did not want to be seen to be telling on anyone by saying that I had been given them. 'I did. I am sorry, Mr Bauld, I didn't realise they belonged to you.'

I was hopping on one foot trying to remove the shoes as quickly as possible. Willie regarded me sternly. 'Remember one thing, young Davie,' he instructed.

'Yes, what is that?'

'The name's Willie.' At that, everyone broke into laughter and, from then on, I felt far more relaxed and at home.

There was an air of excitement around the place. In the 1949–50 season, Hearts had finished third in the League and in the following two seasons we were still close in at fourth. In 1951–52, only Motherwell prevented us from reaching the Scottish Cup final for the first time in many years. To top it all, Willie Bauld was playing for Scotland. With Conn, Bauld and Wardhaugh up front, the goals were flying in and the team was generally playing better with each season; I felt it would be very hard for me to break through. Although I had great determination and was single-minded in my ambition, I was only too aware that not everyone made it. By this time, Hearts had let go of my brother Tommy.

Towards the end of the 1952–53 season, I was finally picked to play for the reserves at Montrose. The game ended in a 6–6 draw and I can remember very little about the match except the sheer exhaustion I felt afterwards. Just like when I had met England as a boy and when I had first played for Newtongrange Star, I really felt the step-up in class and fitness levels. I think I tried too hard and, even though I knew I should not go for every ball and involve myself in every piece of action, I couldn't stop myself. The result was a worn-out teenager who gave the appearance of being a loose cannon.

My home reserve debut against East Fife a week later was better. We won 2–1 for a start and I was more settled in my game.

A reporter remarked that my tackling, interventions and distribution gave evidence of great promise. That was enough; I was in the reserves and played out the rest of the season with them. Nevertheless, I knew that my fitness left something to be desired and that really the only way to improve that was to train regularly with the rest of the chaps, but this was impossible whilst working from 7.30 a.m. to 5.30 p.m. for Mr McIntosh. On Saturdays, I was playing and on Sundays – well, Sundays are the day of rest. Now I was in the reserves, Mr McIntosh was warming towards me and maybe he was beginning to think that perhaps I did have a career with his beloved club. It was by no means clear at that point. The first team finished fourth again and had reached the semi-final of the Scottish Cup, this time succumbing only to the mighty Rangers. Also the man whose position I understudied, Davie Laing, was on top form.

It was a week before my 19th birthday in the November of the 1953–54 season when I made my debut in the first team. Fate had played a hand. I was playing well in the reserves, but it took an injury to Davie Laing to get me elevated. The match was against Clyde at Tynecastle and 16,000 fans witnessed us lose 1–2 in a close game, with Jimmy Wardhaugh scoring our goal. Yet again, I was wrong-footed by the step-up in class, although this time it was more mental than physical. In the reserves, we might be planning one or two moves ahead, but in the first team we were thinking several in advance. The Clyde forwards outpassed me and on several occasions I was left looking stupid as their left-winger spirited past me. I knew it was not a good performance and so did Tommy Walker. He dropped me. Still, it was a landmark. I had played for Hearts. Mum and Dad had been there to watch me and all was not doom and gloom. Had I had a sweetheart, I may have taken her out to the cinema that night to celebrate the occasion. We'd have watched *The African Queen* with Humphrey Bogart and Katherine Hepburn. Or we could have gone dancing. Frankie Laine was number one in the charts with 'Answer Me'. It was also at number two, but this time by David Whitfield. We were a very unsophisticated record-buying public at the time. My girlfriend would have been wearing shoes with the new stiletto heels that were all the rage and she would have had to remove them to dance. Sadly, she did not exist.

In my very shy way, I was trying to make contact with the opposite sex. I didn't come across many girls or women at Lawrence McIntosh or through playing football. With four boys at home, we were a very male-orientated household. Yet a feeling inside me told me I was missing out on something. This tends to happen to most young men sooner or later. I'd go along with a pal or two to the Edinburgh Palais on a Saturday night, where we would stand and shuffle our feet awkwardly as we watched the female population of Edinburgh and its environs dance the night away. We'd be dressed in our best suits (our only suits) and try hard to appear relaxed as we tapped our feet to the big bands that rotated at the Palais.

I was there one Saturday in February 1954, all spruced up after a reserve game at Tynecastle. (Worryingly, Tommy Walker had not seen fit to try me again in the first team since my Clyde debut three months earlier.) The dancing was reaching its peak and I was standing about on the fringes of the throng, doubtless thinking about our visit to Queen of the South reserves the following week. The jitterbugging stopped and the floor cleared as the band struck up in anticipation of 'Ladies' Choice'. This was a potentially terrifying juncture in the evening when the girls scoured the dance floor (unless they had already decided) and then selected a boy they wished to be their partner. It was terrifying because there were more ladies than men and nobody wanted to be one of the forlorn-looking chaps left standing a little embarrassed and adrift, having not been approached. I normally felt the call of nature around then, but happily this night I was too engrossed in my own footballing thoughts.

'Can you quickstep?'

I snapped out of my reverie and saw the most beautiful young girl smiling sweetly at me. We danced and I confessed to my fear of Ladies' Choice.

'It's worse for the girls,' she pointed out. 'Imagine how it is if the man says no.'

I hadn't considered that.

51

Isobel Dixon came from a small mining village called Whitecraig, just south of Musselburgh, which in turn lies just outside Edinburgh. She told me she came from a family of boys and that they all supported Hibernian. I kept quiet. In fact, I did not mention I played football at all. As far as she was concerned, I was a joiner. I wasn't being deliberately secretive, I just didn't believe that me telling her I played for Hearts reserves would particularly impress. We were immediately besotted with one another and after a few weeks started to 'walk out', which in effect meant staying in at one another's house five nights a week.

Another reason I probably didn't mention my footballing career to Isobel was that I wasn't sure whether I was going to have one or not. I had absolute faith in Tommy Walker's judgement and if he didn't feel that I was first-team material then he was probably right. On my part, I would not be happy ploughing my trade in the reserves. I would rather not be in the water, if I were only treading it. On top of this, the slog of working a long day at McIntosh's and then rolling up at Tynecastle in the evening for training was wearing me out. I made the decision that I would quit Hearts at the end of the season. Whether I would have ever really acted on this decision, I will never know.

One Wednesday evening, I was in my overalls with my tools slung over my shoulder. I'd had a hard day's joining and was off to Tynecastle to watch the boys in action. I may have been getting disillusioned with myself, but I was still in love with the club. We were due to play Hamilton Academical. As I approached the ground, Freddie Glidden, a first-team player, caught me up.

'Davie, John Harvey is looking for you. You should hurry.'

John was our trainer and I wasted no time in finding him. He told me to get ready, that I was playing that very evening. I really had no idea. Neither Tommy Walker nor anyone else had given me any inkling that they were thinking of giving me another run out. It all happened so fast. Less than 150 minutes after being told I was playing, we were 3–0 victors. I had played in the same team as King Willie Bauld for the first time. He had scored and the 13,000 crowd were delighted. I had a good game and the papers thought so too. One journalist said I was 'top of the bill' and another commented, 'it will be hard to keep Davie Mackay in the reserves'. He was right. Injury apart, I was never out of the first team again.

The following Saturday we travelled northwards to Aberdeen, where we narrowly lost by a single goal. Because of the distance, I was unable to make the Saturday night at the Palais. Apparently, Isobel asked my friend where I was and he said I was in Aberdeen. She was curious to know what I would be doing all the way up there.

'Playing for Hearts, of course,' he explained. She laughed her head off.

We won away to Clyde in the last match of the season and ended up finishing second to Celtic in the Championship. There was a five-point difference, but Hearts had dropped seven points in their last six games to allow Celtic to pip us. Nevertheless, it was our best finish for many a year and the team was very much looking forward to the 1954–55 season. The Terrible Trio were playing better and better, Jim Souness was dazzling on the wing, my old pal Willie Duff had also broken into the team and Freddie Glidden, John Cumming and I were gelling well in the defensive midfield. There was a general air of excited anticipation around Tynecastle, but first of all there was the end-of-season tour of South Africa to look forward to. I had picked up an injury in a game against my bogey side, Clyde, and it looked for a while that I may not have been fit to travel, but was waved through at the last moment. My spirits were soaring; my 'walking out' with Isobel had developed into 'going steady', I was a first-team player at Hearts, the team were buzzing and now I was flying off with them on the Comet to a far-off land. The Comet was the plane of the future, superseded by Concorde, which now, bizarrely, is the plane of the past with nothing to succeed it. Perhaps they will revive the Comet.

It was my first experience of overseas travel. My first plane, my first boat, my first hotel (besides the St Pancras place), my first black person. There were no people of Afro-Caribbean or Asian origin settled in Edinburgh in those days. At least, not in the parts I visited. There were very few elsewhere in the British Isles. The only black faces that were instantly recognisable would have been boxer Joe Louis and musician Nat King Cole. It was a very different world. I was not aware of apartheid. I cannot recall thinking it wrong, or even odd, that in the stadiums in which we played, the black spectators were penned in all together in one enclosure. I thought they just liked to stand with one another. It didn't strike me as odd, either, that in a country with a huge black majority that every team we played, including the national one, was completely made up of whites.

Our hosts treated us very well, taking us out to see the sights: the Voortrekker Monument in Pretoria, a diamond mine, game reserves and wine-growing areas. There were no trips out from Cape Town to visit Robben Island then. I managed to get myself injured again, this time when I stubbed my toe in training, and was out for a couple of the games. I did play in a match where Tommy Walker played all defenders and we won 4–0. I was then in the team for the big one – against the South African national side – in Durban, where the final score was 2–1. In this game, I went up for a cross with the goalkeeper and, understandably, he confused my head with the ball and punched me full on in the ear. My head was ringing and I was more than a little alarmed to find my ear bleeding. A little later, I took another knock to the ear, which caused the drum to bleed even more, and had to be carried off to hospital. I spent the next three days under the careful eyes of doctors whilst the lads finished the tour. The hospital was as luxurious as the hotel and I really enjoyed my stay. The tour was useful, for me at least, because I established a relationship with my teammates, most of whom were older. I was playing well and my period as the club's equivalent of the tea boy was over.

The only down side about my trip to the other side of the world was being away from Isobel and our parting made me realise that I was seriously in love with her. I was also aware that any time now our relationship would be tested by a more permanent enforced absence on my part. My call-up papers would soon plop through the letter box and this would mean two years of National Service in the army. I did not resent this at all. It wasn't like I had been unfairly selected. We all did it. Rich and poor. Scottish and

English. Tall and short. The government of the day was not taking any chances, having experienced two world wars in twenty-five years, the end of the second one only a short decade earlier. Nobody wanted to be caught on the hop.

It is a cliché, I know, and a much maligned one at that, but I do believe that National Service made a man of you; if we still operated such a system today, I think we'd have far fewer problems than we currently do. Besides all the discipline stuff – and people react to that in different ways – if nothing else, it took young men off the streets at a time when their physical and mental development dictated they would be most predisposed to getting themselves into trouble. It was a mistake to abandon it. Such an opinion is generally scoffed at nowadays, but just because a view is not fashionable or politically correct, does that mean it should not be aired? I hope not.

When my papers arrived the following year, the government, in its wisdom, decided I had all the qualifications needed to become a Royal Engineer (I suppose there were no Royal Joiners) and sent me to a barracks in Worcester in England. This was the first time I had lived away from Glendevon Park permanently, and from Mum and Dad and my brothers, and although I said earlier I didn't resent it, I was not very happy. I was in, what was to me at that stage, a foreign country and I was spending my time polishing boots and being shouted at. It took time to adjust. However, I was luckier than most because the army had come to an agreement with Hearts Football Club that I would be allowed home every weekend to play football. I would fly back on a Friday night, play for Hearts on a Saturday, see Isobel in the evening and have Sunday lunch with her parents or mine, and then rush to catch the ten o'clock train for Birmingham. Eight hours later, it would arrive and I would then have to travel on to Worcester and ensure I was in camp by eight o'clock. It was all a mad rush.

A young Celtic player by the name of Eric Smith was also stationed at the barracks and we travelled back on the ten o'clock train together. Eric would already be in his carriage when the train pulled into Edinburgh from Glasgow and I would be able to find him by spying the green and white scarf wrapped around the handle.

Literally, the day before I set off for Worcester for the first time on 21 August 1955, I had played against Eric. We had beaten Celtic 2–1 at Parkhead in the League Cup and propelled ourselves to the quarter-finals. Quite a result. The previous Wednesday, I had scored my first senior goal in a League Cup game against Falkirk. We crushed them 6–2 and I shared the goal-sheet with the Terrible Trio. King Willie got two, Jimmy got two and me and Alfie Conn took one each. Although it was my first goal, it put the Trio on a combined total of 400!

The Scottish League Cup did not command the same prestige as the Scottish Cup at that stage, yet it was a trophy worth winning – especially for Hearts, who had not won a bean for half a century. It was played in the opening months of the season and we approached it with gusto and a firm belief that we would win it at least. St Johnstone and Aidrieonians were disposed of in the quarter- and semi-finals respectively, and before we could really think about the strides we had made, we were facing Motherwell in the Scottish League Cup final at Hampden Park on 23 October 1954. A year earlier, I had been languishing in the reserves contemplating my future; now, I was playing at the highest level and was due to compete in my first senior cup final.

Mum didn't go to Hampden Park for the match. Although she and Dad had always turned out to watch and encourage me as a schoolboy, once I graduated to senior football she said she could not watch anymore. She was fearful of the tackling and what might happen to me. She said it made her feel ill and that when she saw me sliding in for a tackle, she was scared I would break a leg or worse. I imagine by worse she was thinking of my neck.

'I'm a footballer, Mum, not a boxer,' I would say. Later in my career, I would discover just how well founded her fears were. Dad still came religiously and was revelling in his son's rise to fame. The rest of the family – and the maroon half of Edinburgh, for that matter – decamped to Hampden for the final. Forty-eight years of hurt were about to come to an end.

It was a fast, furious and entertaining game, and I enjoyed every minute. Motherwell, like us, had a reputation as a good footballing side, even if they were rarely amongst the honours. We defeated them by four goals to two and, fittingly, King Willie Bauld provided three of them; Jimmy Wardhaugh scored the other. At the end of the match, it was like a dam had burst as the Hearts faithful streamed onto the pitch and mobbed and fêted us as heroes. When Bobby Parker, our captain, lifted the Cup high, I can remember thinking that life could not get better. But it did.

We travelled in the team bus back down the Corstorphine Road towards Edinburgh and stopped in the Harp public house. There we drank some beer as we waited for the open-top bus to arrive to take us back into town. By the time we boarded, the ale had begun to affect me (I had only ever drunk a couple of pints before in my entire life). My euphoria was increasing by the minute. As we pulled into Princes Street, the most amazing sight greeted us. Even though the night was cold, thousands of people wrapped in heavy overcoats and scarves were cheering us on and filling the road. I said earlier that the coach was open-topped: a trap door in the roof was a better description and us players scrambled through it, Cup in hands, to milk and absorb the adulation. Most of the players, including myself, were supporters as well, so it was a double victory. As a player, I had won the Cup. As a supporter, my team had won its first trophy in half a century. I had never experienced such bliss.

There was a reception at the North British Hotel, now the Balmoral, and I was immediately plied with celebratory champagne and then whisky. Someone stuffed an enormous cigar in my mouth. I wasn't complaining. I defy anyone, though, to honestly say they enjoyed the taste of whisky the first time they took it. For a boy whose most exotic drink had previously been diluted orange, it tasted sharp, hot and unpleasant. But I could not argue with the warm feeling that rushed from my stomach up to my head. Equally, I had never smoked a cigarette, so the effects of the cigar (and the ones after it) all contributed to my light-headedness. When we left the reception, a few of the younger players and I decided to hit our Saturday night haunt, the Edinburgh Palais. Here, we really could bask in our success, among the ordinary folk of town and our pals and girlfriends. On the door, though, the commissionaires – as they were known in the age before doormen and bouncers were required – told us we were too late to be allowed entry.

'We've just won the Cup with Hearts,' I explained, 'we're all footballers.'

'I don't care if you're all escaped prisoners of war. There's no entry after 9 p.m.'

And that was that. Nobody argued. Next door, though, there was a private party and someone spotted us and invited us in. That's where it all becomes blurred. My next clear memory is of waking up on the settee at Glendevon Park. Beside me was a bucket. An unpleasant smell pervaded the air.

CHAPTER FOUR

Treble

A crowd of 30,000 fans turned up at Tynecastle for our first home match after the League Cup victory and, on a crest of euphoria, we whacked Falkirk 5–3. However, we did not sustain our early season promise completely, going out of the Scottish Cup in the quarter-finals to Aberdeen and ending up fourth in the League. We were not deterred, however, and still felt that better things would come. We were playing good, entertaining football and scoring plenty of goals. From the manager downwards, there was a strong ethos that quality football will out.

Back in the forces, I had been exposed to some of the big, young names in English football when I was selected to play some matches for the army side. I played against and alongside Eddie Coleman, Maurice Setters and Duncan Edwards, and also a young Welsh boy called Cliff Jones. Cliff played dazzlingly out on the wing and I can remember thinking that he would undoubtedly break through in the game. I would never have imagined that we would be winning trophies together for the same team within five years. Eddie, Maurice and Duncan were already established at Manchester United, young as they were. Duncan and Eddie in particular were already famous as leading 'Busby Babes' – the exciting young side built by Scotsman Matt Busby. As most people will remember, Duncan and Eddie were amongst those who perished in the Munich air crash a few short years after I played in the same team as them. For people of my generation, it is one the tragic public events that form desperately sad milestones along the paths of our lives. Munich, Kennedy, Aberfan, Dunblane – the names themselves are enough to re-ignite the emotions felt at the time.

In purely footballing terms, Duncan is generally regarded as the biggest loss of the Munich air disaster and undoubtedly he was an exceptional talent. Indeed, by the time I played with him, he had already debuted for England despite being only 18 years old. He displayed a footballing maturity beyond his years and, had he lived, it may have been him, not Bobby Moore, who captained England to their 1966 World Cup victory. Perhaps they would have won it in 1962? Yet, in my experience of playing with him and watching him, it was Eddie Coleman who had the greatest impact on me. They called him 'Snakehips' because of the way he bodyswerved and nutmegged opponents. He was flamboyant and full of confidence, and he was only a boy. I felt strongly that he would grow into one of England's top talents. He was a delight to watch. It seems an age now since all those boys died. Forever young, they belong to a different time – smeared in Brylcreem and frozen in black-and-white grainy newsreels. Yet, had they lived, they would only just be drawing their pensions today.

Talking of great players, the club had another one coming through at Tynecastle. We opened the 1955–56 season with a 4–0 League Cup win over East Fife, and Alex Young, a wispish centre-forward, bagged his first hat-trick in only his third first-team appearance. Like me, Alex had served his apprenticeship with Newtongrange Star and had done his time in the reserves. For a centre-forward, he was small, but I've seen him out-jump centre-halves who had nearly a foot on him, and then there was the uncanny way he could hang in the air and wait for the ball to come to his head rather than the other way around. It was almost supernatural. With his hair like flakes of gold pasted to his head, his sparkling eyes and classic bone structure, there was something of the Roman emperor about him. The fans called him 'The Golden Vision'. Unless Tommy Walker could accommodate him and the Terrible Trio in the same forward line, Alex threatened the status quo.

A particular landmark occurred in my life on Monday, 12 December 1955. On the Saturday, Hearts had drawn 1–1 away at Falkirk. In the afternoon of the Monday, Isobel and I were married at Haymarket Registry Office and in the evening, fortuitously, it was the Hearts Football Club Christmas dance, so that year it doubled up as our wedding reception. It was a wonderful day that we will always treasure. Some time later, we had the marriage blessed at Our Lady of Loretto in Musselburgh.

My life was now accelerating forward on all fronts. I was playing my best football yet. The press were calling for the international selectors to pick me for the national side. Hearts themselves were going great guns: we had defeated Celtic in the League (although we had lost to Rangers and my boyhood pal, Ralph Brand, played a vital role) and were in the running for the Championship. My pay had risen to £20 a week, although I had now lost my £5 a week from Lawrence McIntosh. Mr McIntosh was pleased with my progress as a Hearts player and had no wish for me to be distracted in any way. We parted company on amicable terms, but I was left with £20 a week, the maximum wage. There was no way any footballer in Scotland or England could legitimately earn any more, except via controlled win-bonuses. 'Soccer slavery', a term coined by Jimmy Hill, who would later campaign down in England for a better deal for players, may have been a bit on the emotive side, but it was a ridiculous situation. At the time, I was still not really sensitive to this side of things even though I had embarked on a marriage and would hopefully soon have a family to support. The fact that I was being paid, handsomely in my opinion, to do something I loved still made me pinch myself every morning. Providing I could offer food and shelter for my wife, I would happily have done it for nothing. In those days, most players felt the same way.

We had been saving our pennies furiously so we could put down a deposit on a house of our own and, at the same time, as an insurance policy, had also registered our names for a corporation house. When we reached the top of the waiting list and were offered a place in Isobel's home town of Whitecraig, we decided to take it. I think it may have been the first time that Isobel worried about my impetuousness when I decided, as there was no immediate use for the savings, I would go out and buy a car. She was not best pleased when I arrived home in a brand spanking new Hillman Minx. Whisky, cigars and new cars. Whatever next?

By March 1956, the quarter-finals of the Scottish Cup were upon us. We had comfortably disposed of Forfar Athletic and Stirling Albion in earlier rounds and felt that we could beat Glasgow Rangers even though it was generally considered they were the best team in Scotland at the time. Nearly 50,000 spectators jammed into Tynecastle to see us crush them 4–0, the goals coming from Willie Bauld (2), Alfie Conn and our young winger, Ian Crawford. The semi-final against Raith Rovers was to be held at Hibernian's Easter Road ground and it should have been a formality: our chance to win our first Scottish Cup final for 50 years seemed assured. In the event, Raith held us to a draw in the first match but we overcame them 3–0 in the replay. Ian Crawford found the net again but, just to remind everyone that the Terrible Trio were still functioning effectively, Jimmy Wardhaugh provided the other two.

The final against Celtic at Hampden Park was much anticipated. Again, we felt we could win it. At the time, we feared Celtic less than Rangers. We had beaten them and drawn with them in our two League matches. We were the underdogs, but knew we shouldn't be. Our team had reached that wonderful stage where we had that elusive blend of age and experience, with a number of players precisely at their career peaks. It was a stable line-up and we knew each other and our respective strengths and weaknesses inside out. Tommy Walker's personality and ethos had been stamped on us. Without overtly saying it, he had taught us to believe in ourselves without slipping into arrogance or complacency.

In the run-up to the final, we could think of nothing else and were like tigers straining at the leash. In one match, we walked over Dunfermline 5–0 and I managed to fire in two of the goals. In the very last game before the final, Falkirk were on the end of our unbridled enthusiasm and conceded eight goals to us. In the wider footballing world, it was all happening in Manchester. Matt Busby's young United side had won the League and City had won the FA Cup final at Wembley against Birmingham. Their goalkeeper, Bert Trautmann, had played on with an injury that was diagnosed afterwards as a small case of a broken neck. In the wider, wider world, Rocky Marciano had just retired undefeated as heavyweight boxing champion of the world, film star Grace Kelly broke male hearts the world over by marrying Prince Rainier of Monaco and the Archbishop of Canterbury condemned the government's new wheeze to raise indirect tax by launching Premium Bonds. We weren't in that wider world. We were playing Celtic at Hampden.

Our skipper Bobby Parker was out for the match with a cartilage injury and Freddie Glidden took on the captaincy. Alex Young, who was now adapting to any role in the forward line, was in the team along with the Terrible Trio. Ian Crawford joined them on the wing and John Cumming and I were the wing-halves. Willie Duff still patrolled between the sticks and his full-backs that day were Tam McKenzie, the oldest and most experienced man in the team, and Bobby Kirk. An incredible 133,000 fans squashed into Hampden Park – the largest crowd Hearts had ever played in front of and, I am sure, ever will.

Ian Crawford, who had only recently been given a free transfer from Hibernian, blasted in our first goal from 20 yards after running on to an Alfie Conn pass. At half-time, we led 1–0. Tommy Walker was calm and told us not to make the mistake of just defending and attempting to merely hang on to the lead. I expect we had been doing this subconsciously. I, for one, was terrified at the prospect of losing our lead. Eric Smith was on the Celtic side and, had we lost, travelling back to camp with him and then the merciless ribbing when we got there would have been unbearable. Acting on Tommy's advice, we attacked Celtic from the second-half whistle and were rewarded within three minutes with another goal from Ian Crawford. This was surely his finest moment. Despite Tommy's instruction, we did then play a game of containment and took no chances. Alfie Conn, though, put the final out of Celtic's reach in the 80th minute with a shot from 15 yards. The reality was that Celtic did not play well and were never a serious threat.

We were lucky that Charlie Tully didn't have a good game. Outside of Hearts, he was my hero. Unless you are a student of Irish or Scottish football or, of course, a Celtic fan, his name may not be familiar, but Charlie was, and still is, a legend at Parkhead. An Irish winger with similarities to Jimmy Johnstone (who came later), he was a delight to watch – always giving value for money with his impudent play and wonderful box of tricks. In a game against Falkirk in the 1951 Scottish Cup, he did the one-in-a-million and scored direct from an in-swinging corner. Celtic were trailing by two goals at the time. The crowd went berserk when the referee disallowed the goal for some minor infringement off the ball and ordered Charlie to retake the corner. He scored again the second time and, amazingly, in exactly the same way. Celtic went on to win the match 3–2. After the disappointing final against us, he achieved immortality as the magician in the Celtic side that butchered the archenemy Rangers in the following year's League Cup final. The following poem was written by Daniel McDonagh about Charlie:

CHARLIE TULLY

When a Belfast boy wore football boots,
He stored a lion's heart,
He would part the waves of the River Clyde
As he walked to Celtic Park.

How the fans would hurry,
To the gates of Paradise,
To see this boy from Ireland
Play with a smile in his eyes.

64

His style was immaculate,
When he played left wing for the 'Tic',
As Falkirk fans remember
His goal, curled from a corner kick.

The ghosts of Hampden still cheer the game,
That was played in '57,
When Tully and the Celtic team
Beat the Rangers by a score of seven.

We took a bus back into Edinburgh on the same route as we had the previous season after our League Cup victory. The crowd cheered us as we crawled into Princes Street again, but this time there were even more people and they were even more jubilant. A dinner was held in the Charlotte Rooms in South Charlotte Street and this time I was careful with my alcohol intake. In the morning, I was happy to see that a number of the national newspapers had named me as man of the match, but I felt that honour should have gone to John Cumming, who cut his head badly in the first half after a clash of heads. He had continued to play in the second half, blood streaming down his face throughout after the wound opened up again, before eventually having to throw in the towel. John was a hard man and in training we endeavoured to toughen up one another further by charging each other from a distance and colliding our shoulders and chests. There was not a ball in sight. The other lads said it was like watching two fighting stags lock horns.

If the League Cup victory in 1954 signalled a turn in Hearts' fortunes, the Scottish Cup victory over Celtic and our continued presence in the Championship race woke people up to what an excellent side we had become. Then, as now, and especially outside of Scotland, there was a perception that all other Scottish football clubs were a mere supporting cast in the duel between Celtic and Rangers. At Tynecastle, we believed our best had yet to come and, at the start of the 1956–57 season, there was a resolve to win the League and a hope that we could win the Double.

John Cumming, Jimmy Wardhaugh and Alfie Conn had all

recently been capped by their country. Willie Bauld had been capped, but not for some time, and there was a groundswell of opinion that Alex Young and I would soon be called up for international duty. Many people in Edinburgh thought that selectors should be less cautious and just play the Terrible Trio before they became too old and broke up.

In February 1957, I got my first sure indication that a full international call-up was imminent when I was selected and appointed captain of the Scottish Under-23 side for a match against England to be played at Ibrox Park. This was a tremendous honour, although I must admit a slight shiver went down my spine as I contemplated meeting Johnny Haynes again. He was no longer the boy who had mentally scarred me nearly ten years earlier; like me, he had become a man. Unlike me, he was by then a full international and very famous all over. I was pleased that Ian Crawford, my match-winning teammate, was also in the side. The match was a hard, physical one and I thought we did well to hold the English to a goal-less draw. But I was unprepared for the onslaught I received from some quarters of the press, especially the English national newspapers. They accused me of being dirty in the way I attempted to contain Haynes and England's young forward, Terry Dyson of Spurs. I had stuck to Johnny like glue and was uncompromising in my tackling generally. But then I always was. The referee had seen no reason to caution or discipline me in any way. I was upset by the coverage, having only experienced thus far a sympathetic, supportive and appreciative press in Scotland. My admiration for Johnny Haynes increased immeasurably when he stepped into the row and issued the following statement to the media:

> I wish every player I met tackled as fairly as Dave Mackay.
> I thought he had an excellent game. He got stuck in, but always went for the ball.
>
> I am amazed that there should be any quibbling about his play. For my part, he is a quick, hard tackler who sets out to give everything he has got. That's his job and he did it without the slightest suggestion of unfair tactics. Anyone who says anything else is talking nonsense.

Domestically, our focus on the League Championship was paying off and Rangers and ourselves were neck and neck, and ten points clear of the chasing pack. On the third-last game of the season, we played each other at Tynecastle and it was clear that if one side prevailed, the Championship was almost surely going to follow. Rangers had already put us out of the Scottish Cup and in front of a 50,000 crowd they managed to overcome us by a single goal: the Scottish League Championship was to elude us yet again.

The season was not a disappointment, though. Morale was still high. We had played great and rewarding football. We had nearly won the Championship by playing high-scoring, high-octane football. The forward line of Wardhaugh, Young, Bauld, Conn and Crawford was irresistible. Tommy Walker explained calmly that patience is a virtue and that the Championship would surely come. I was on a high anyway. Our first child had been born by then. It was a wonderful, healthy boy. I was so happy and proud to continue the Mackay family line that, like everyone else, I bowed to tradition and called him David.

My Under-23 game for Scotland must have registered, despite the bad press I received in some quarters over my tackling, because I was selected to join the full Scottish squad in May 1957 to play a World Cup qualifier against Spain. This was a tremendous honour, although I really did not expect to play in such an important fixture. Still, it boded well for the future. I don't know who selected me because the international side did not have a manager then. It was all done by committee. No one could take the credit when we did well and nobody could be blamed when we played badly. It was handy in a way because there was no manager to get the sack, but it is a rather an unsatisfactory way to run a team. Any team.

I remember soaking in a bath at the Philip II Hotel, El-Escorial, Madrid. Hotels remained a novelty to me and I made the most of whatever was on offer. Neatly wrapped soap. Bubbles. Coloured shampoo. Fluffy towels. Yes, please. I even read the Bible that was in the bedside drawer. Bobby Evans tapped on the door and I called him in.

'Dave!' he squealed. 'Congratulations. You're in the team on Sunday.'

That was the good news. The bad news was that he and I were replacing George Young and Ian McColl of Glasgow Rangers. This would be an unpopular decision. George was a colossus. He'd been playing since before the war (the second one) and was a genuine Scottish hero. He was the first player to achieve 50 international caps. These days, they'd probably call him the guv'nor. He was by then 35 years of age and it was generally accepted that this tour would be his last and that the Spanish World Cup tie would be his final international match. Like Alan Shearer decades later, his stature was such that he could dictate when he retired. Or so he thought. There was absolutely no need to change the team anyway. Scotland had won their last three games convincingly – one of those games being against Spain. It was the sort of decision only a faceless committee could come up with.

George would never play for his country again and his relations with the Scottish game were forever soured. Our own camp was also split by the decision. Some felt it was a mark of disrespect to leave George and Ian out. Some felt it was foolhardy. Others believed that if we were to have any chance of success in the following year's World Cup finals in Sweden, we'd have to blood some youngsters. Therefore, my international debut was marred by considerable ill-feeling among players, fans and journalists – yet before I ran out onto the pitch, George Young himself grabbed my elbow and said some very nice things to me. He was a gentleman.

Jimmy Greaves has a record of scoring on all of his debuts. I seemed to have a record of marking my debuts by playing poorly. I was terrible. Bobby Evans had far more experience than me and he advised me not to play my familiar game of sliding tackles and charging defenders.

'You'll need to stay on your feet against this lot,' he counselled, with considerable understatement. As usual, I took no notice. This Spanish side contained three of the greatest footballers of all time: Di Stefano, Kubala and Gento, and they were in a different league to me. It was hard not to stand open-mouthed and admire their balletic poise and inch-perfect passes; their absolute telepathy. I looked and felt like an old Shire horse trotting up alongside Shergar. In the second half, I took a knock on the ankle that didn't help, but the truth is I was outclassed, outplayed and, in all probability, out of the international team. We lost 4–1, but if it had not been for a superhuman performance from Tommy Younger in goal, it could have got to double figures.

The Bernabéu stadium where the match was played was Alfredo Di Stefano's home ground. His Real Madrid side were truly the Kings of Europe, winning the European Cup five times during his tenure at the club. He and Kubala had transformed Spanish football, although strangely neither player was actually Spanish. Di Stefano was born in Argentina and Kubala was born in Hungary. Di Stefano actually played for three countries: Argentina, Columbia and Spain. So for those people who think footballers picking and choosing which country they play for, or using the grounds that they had an auntie who once went on a charabang trip to Llandudno as the premise for their Welshness, is a new phenomenon, think again.

After the game, one of the established players could see how bad I was feeling. He was a self-confident man who didn't mince his words. He had been playing in England for some time with Preston North End and was in the same team as the English legend Tom Finney. It was like he read my mind. I was thinking that my international career was as good as over. That I was competent, perhaps good, on the Scottish domestic stage, but I had reached my limit.

'Dinnae worry, Davie, you'll have another chance. Mark my words. The best is yet to come.' Thomas Henderson Docherty patted my head and jumped into the bath.

Despite what Tommy Docherty said, my international career was over for the time being. It would be a year before I got that second chance and a year is an age in the life of an ambitious young footballer. If it was not for what happened next at home, with Hearts, I might have become depressed. In the 1957–58 season, Heart of Midlothian Football Club positively exploded.

All that pent-up talent, drive and potential burst forth. From the off, we knew it was our destiny and there would be no stopping us. To mark my discharge from the army (no more 800-mile round trips every weekend and therefore a greater presence at Tynecastle), Tommy Walker appointed me captain and this made me more proud than anything that had gone before. Even being capped by my country. Wee Davie Mackay, captain of the Hearts. Can you believe it? This was real Roy of the Rovers stuff and I became doubly determined to help supply the perfect ending to my personal fairy tale.

We opened the season by smashing Dundee 6–0 at Tynecastle. Then we travelled to Aidrie and put seven past them. Back home we easily despatched arch rivals Hibernian 3–1 and then scored a ridiculous nine against a shell-shocked East Fife. Aberdeen and Rangers conceded seven goals to us between them, before we lost our one and only League game to Clyde (who else?) in the November. The entire season was a feast of goals and football being played at its finest. Even I managed a hat-trick in a 9–0 drubbing of Falkirk. I don't think a team had ever won a Championship in such style, with such panache and with so many goals. As Lloyd Grossman might say: 'Let's look at the evidence.' We beat Rangers and Celtic each time we played them. We lost only one game and drew only four. We scored 132 goals and conceded only 29. We amassed a record 62 points. The second-placed club, Rangers, only managed 49. Jimmy Wardhaugh scored 28 goals, whilst Jimmy Murray found the net 27 times and Alex Young, now firmly established in the side, notched up 24. I got a record (for me) twelve, including five penalties. It was unbelievable.

I missed the last few matches of this glorious, historic season through another foot injury, but this did not detract too much, such was the excitement. By the time I broke a bone in my foot, the Championship was as good as won and I knew the rest of the lads would not trip up. The only slightly sad note for me was that this 1958 triumph also marked the end of the Terrible Trio. Although Jimmy Wardhaugh had been our top scorer, Willie Bauld and Alfie Conn had only managed 14 games between them. Mind you, they still produced nine goals. Injury and the form of others had kept them out of the team. The following season the partnership ended officially with the departure of Alfie Conn to Raith Rovers.

It was my finest moment at Hearts and in Scotland. Raising the League flag at Tynecastle for the first time in 61 years really was the stuff of dreams and I had been the 23-year-old skipper of the team that had done it. Wise, kind Tommy Walker said some lovely things to me; my local community made such a fuss; the supporters idolised us and the press saluted us. Everywhere I went people stopped me and shook my hand or asked for an autograph or just said, 'Well done, Dave.' Whoever complained about the pressures of fame? I loved every minute.

To cap it all, I was voted Player of the Year by the *Sunday Mail*'s column 'Rex on Sunday', a prestigious accolade at the time, and I went to the Usher Hall in Edinburgh to collect my award. That was a great honour and totally unexpected. I still viewed myself as a new kid on the block.

Hearts' momentum continued into the 1958–59 season, although Standard Liege dumped us out of the European Cup at the first hurdle. Before we could get used to the idea of being champions, we found ourselves at Hampden again on 25 October 1958 in the final of the Scottish League Cup. Our opponents this time were Partick Thistle and, curiously, some commentators thought we would not beat them. Hearts romped home in front of 60,000 supporters to beat Thistle 5–1. In the twilight of his illustrious career, King Willie scored two of the goals to give us our fourth trophy in as many years. As captain, I lifted my second Cup and drank in the atmosphere as we drove down Princes Street on the victory bus on what was now a familiar route. We were playing well enough to retain the Championship. There was the Scottish Cup coming up. I could smell a Treble. I wanted to be the captain of not only the finest Hearts team in history, but also the finest Scottish team in history. There was still much to go for. I would never have dreamt it then as I stood on the bus waving and cheering with the people of Edinburgh, but other people had different plans.

PART TWO

Spurs

CHAPTER FIVE

Taking the High Road

A year after my disappointing international debut against Spain, I was recalled to the national squad to travel to Sweden for the 1958 World Cup finals. Despite the defeat to Di Stefano and co., and without me (maybe this was why), the national side had managed to qualify for the final stages of the biggest football competition in the world. The preparations were shambolic and we ended up competing on the biggest stage without a manager. Sensibly, Matt Busby had been appointed Scottish team manager and everyone felt that, at last, our country was taking its football seriously; that Matt was capable of moulding what was undoubtedly a pool of good players into a serious world-beating side, even though he already had a day job – no, he didn't work for Lawrence McIntosh, he was the manager of Manchester United. Tragically, the aforementioned Munich air disaster happened on 6 February 1958 and Matt had an altogether more serious battle to fight. Why the Scottish footballing authorities did not replace him is beyond me. Can you imagine an international side being allowed to travel to the World Cup finals without a manager nowadays?

As it happened, Tommy Docherty filled the vacuum as best he could. He was merely a player, with no official sanction. He was not even the captain and was not selected to play in any of the games, but in times of crisis, leaders emerge. They have to. We finished bottom of our group after losing to Paraguay and France and drawing with Yugoslavia, and I only played in the 2–1 defeat to the French. Jimmy Murray of Hearts scored Scotland's opening goal in the finals. We were not shamed in the tournament: we played some good football and in some of the matches were unlucky not to win or draw, but we were just not good enough. My point earlier about the poor preparation and lack of guidance was not by way of an excuse. It is a fact that we went with no manager and only 13 players! Had we had taken a squad, had we employed a manager and invested in some weeks of preparation, it is hard to believe that we would not have done better than we did.

The 1958 World Cup finals, though, were a success for these islands of ours in other ways. It was the first and last time that England, Scotland, Wales and Northern Ireland have all qualified for the final stages together. Remarkably, although England and Scotland failed to get out of their groups, Wales and Northern Ireland made it through to the quarter-finals. Wales only succumbed to the eventual winners, Brazil, who showcased for the first time their boy genius – Pelé. The Irish, led by the mercurial Danny Blanchflower, finally went out to France, the country that had put paid to our hopes. Wonderful performances from both countries.

I had a pleasant surprise when I was selected to play against Wales in the Home International Championship later in the year. When I arrived at our hotel in Cardiff, I was puzzled when Matt Busby told me I was rooming on my own and asked me to dump my bags and come downstairs to the foyer to see him for a chat. He was weak and frail, having suffered terrible injuries in the air crash. The fact that he was not only back managing Manchester United in such a short time but had now also resumed control of the national side was incredible. It was surely too much for him. Matt told me that he was appointing me team captain and my chest swelled with pride. Captains are normally senior in years and have been long established in a side. I was just 23 years old and playing only my third international game. Matt could see what I was thinking. Tommy Docherty, then playing at Arsenal, and Bobby Collins of Everton were both in the team and far more experienced and respected than I was.

'Davie, you are the man for the job. Be in no doubt. You are hungry. You never admit defeat. You inspire those around you and you have many years ahead of you. I want to build this Scotland side around you. You are an old head on young shoulders.'

I was extremely flattered and proud. I knew Matt was an admirer of mine – he had always been most encouraging when we had met in the past and I had read good things he had said about me in the press – but I had no idea of the extent of his regard for me. I felt he hinted that he would like to sign me for Manchester United, but there was no definite approach. It was best left unsaid. He knew I was Hearts through and through and he knew it was all happening at Hearts. Playing football in England was not on my radar.

Of course, I agreed to the captaincy.

'Oh, and by the way,' added Matt, 'in the event of a penalty, I want you to take it.' I nodded. 'Also, if Bill Brown [our Dundee goalkeeper at the time] becomes injured, I want you to deputise.' I nodded. I would have peeled the oranges if he had asked. He hadn't finished.

'And Davie, in the event of a penalty, I don't want you to side-foot it. I want you to blast it into the corner of the net. Is that understood?' I wasn't sure why he laboured that point. I had missed penalties at Hearts, but I can't imagine there were more than two or three over my entire career. He had either spotted something in training or he was psychic.

'Finally, Dave, in the event that you have to deputise in goal and a ball comes over, do not rise to the temptation to punch the ball away. Catch it, Davie. Catch it.'

Matt fielded an experimental team with four players making their debuts: John Grant, Bill Toner, David Herd and Denis Law. Denis was only 18 years old and was already receiving rave reviews in the English game at Huddersfield Town. He was good and he knew it, but not big-headed in any way. He was a cheeky chappie who could see the fun in everything and his general good humour and mischievousness was infectious. We became pals straight away. I was not surprised that he became both one of the most admired forwards of his generation and one of greatest Scottish footballers ever. You would be surprised how many ex-professionals rate Denis as the best player they competed against or alongside when asked in private, and they remember just who he played with.

The Welsh side we faced were no mugs. The legendary giant, John Charles, was not in the team but Ivor Allchurch and his brother Len were, along with Terry Medwin of Spurs, Mel Hopkins and Roy Vernon. We played an excellent game of football, winning comfortably 3–0. Denis scored on his debut and Bobby Collins and Graham Leggat made up the others. We were awarded a penalty too and, as I stepped up to take it, I puzzled even myself by side-footing it with the flat of my foot. I couldn't look over at Matt and to this day I have no idea why I ignored his instruction. It just felt the right thing to do at the time. Later in the game, Bill Brown took a nasty knock in an aerial clash and was forced to receive treatment off the field. I deputised in goal. This was becoming spooky. I managed to collect a few balls and stop a couple of shots, but my heart sank as I rushed forward to catch a ball and realised that it was sailing over my head. My instinct had been to punch it, but I remembered Matt's words and stopped myself. The loss of those vital micro-seconds, though, caused me to miss it. I looked forlornly over my shoulder to watch the inevitable. Never fear, the boy wonder, Denis Law, was standing on the line grinning as he cleared the ball away. After the game, Matt was happy: his experiment had worked. He said nothing to me about the penalty or the goalkeeping error but shook his head as if to say 'tut, tut' and then broke into a fatherly smile. Nowadays, players sit down with managers and replay matches on video machines so they can discuss tactics and maybe go over where they went wrong. To this day, I strongly feel that Matt had somehow watched that match before it was played and had run through it in advance.

On Guy Fawkes Night, we played the other World Cup heroes at Hampden and I retained my captaincy. It was an entertaining game as we drew 2–2 with Northern Ireland. They had the legendary Jimmy McIlroy of Burnley and their future manager Billy Bingham in the side, but it was Danny Blanchflower who really impressed me that day. He reminded me of a Continental, like those I had seen on my debut against Spain. His penetrating passing and his ability to slow or speed up the game was breathtaking. He saw space before it was there. I did not know it then, but having played alongside Bill Brown in the Scottish team and against Terry Medwin, Terry Dyson and Cliff Jones, I was slowly but surely being exposed to my future teammates.

Back at Tynecastle, things were looking good. With the League Cup under our belts, it was Rangers and us slogging it out again for the Championship. I picked up another foot injury in a match just before Christmas and was out of action until February 1959. The foot was becoming a worry now. I had missed the end of the previous season because of it and then a chunk of that season. I felt that there wasn't anything inherently wrong with my foot and that each injury had been due to bad luck or carelessness on my part. I had not seen it as a pattern or a threat. Perhaps not everyone at Tynecastle shared this view.

I was fit in time to play against Rangers at Ibrox when they put us out of the Scottish Cup, but we were still neck and neck in the League, therefore a Double was still very much on the cards. On 18 February, we played a League match against Partick Thistle and they were able to exact their revenge for the League Cup final defeat. As we traipsed off the pitch, angry that we had dropped a vital two points, I tried to buck Willie Bauld up. He had not had a great game. This would be the last time we played on the same pitch together. On the Saturday, we were at home to Raith Rovers and we won 2–1. I scored my 29th and final goal for Hearts.

On Saturday, 7 March 1959 we entertained Queen of the South. A 12,000-strong crowd saw us win 2–1, with Jimmy Murray and George Thomson on the score sheet. George, Johnny Hamilton and Alex Young were forming the core of a great new Hearts side and, as captain at the age of 24, I thought I was at the heart of the

79

new side. Sad as I was at the eventual demise of the Terrible Trio and the passing of some of the older players, I identified as strongly with the future as I did with the past. But that relatively pedestrian match with Queen of the South would be my last for Heart of Midlothian Football Club. I wish I had known it. During the week, I damaged my foot in training (again) and was on the sidelines for the match against Motherwell. When I left the lads in the changing-rooms that afternoon, it was the last time I would be with them as a colleague. Within 24 hours, my life would change dramatically and for ever.

Sundays for my family were spent relaxing. Isobel, young David, little Derek, my second son, born in 1958, and I would rise a little later than normal and leisurely hop in the car and drive from Whitecraig over to Glendevon Park to spend the afternoon with my family. Mum and Dad had a new television and it was very much a family pastime to gather around the box in the corner of the room and devour everything that was on offer. By today's standards, that was not much. The national anthem, played at the end of broadcasting each night, ensured you did not forget it was your bedtime. It is difficult to convey now just how exciting it was to have access to a television for the first time. Besides dancing, the highlight of our social lives would be to visit the cinema and when the cinema effectively came to us, in our homes, we could not believe our good fortune. Choice was limited at first, with just one BBC channel and that offering only a test card for large swathes of the waking hours, but when ITV came along in the mid-'50s, the race to entertain and capture the audience began in earnest. Us early viewers became as wrapped up in the world of TV as our parents had earlier with films and the world of Hollywood. We laughed at *I Love Lucy* and *Hancock*, sat on the edge of our seats during *Dragnet* and the more homely *Dixon of Dock Green* – I even enjoyed and remembered each new advertisement as they started to appear on the commercial channel. We learnt that we would never be alone with a Strand cigarette, that the best peas came from Farrows, chimpanzees adored tea and that no smoke would get in our eyes if we used Esso Blue paraffin to heat our homes.

This particular Sunday, we had eaten our roast and settled down to talk football. There would have been nothing on TV, as in those days the broadcasters assumed most people would be at church and they would not want to discourage the population from such a custom. Having digested our dinners and chatted through the good and bad of Hearts and Scottish football, normally we'd have settled down on the settee to watch *Sunday Night at the London Palladium* before heading off home. The *Palladium* was undoubtedly the television highlight of the week. A real-life music-hall and variety show in your own lounge presented at the time by Tommy Trinder. It seemed to last the whole evening and every week boasted the top stars of the time with often an American singing legend or comedian as top of the bill. Sometimes we would not really know who the top of the bill act was, but if they were big stars in America we obediently assumed they were the best. At the end, all the guests would stand on a revolving stage and wave goodbye. We became so engrossed, it was hard not to wave back.

The telephone rang. It stood in the hallway on a small table, black and shiny and in splendid isolation. When it rang, we all started and looked at one another. Then Mum got up and stepped into the hall and answered it – slowly and deliberately. In the next room everyone remained quiet. Not so we could eavesdrop, but out of a sense of politeness. Telephone interruptions were special then. I can recall Mum telling me that a neighbour, who had acquired a telephone earlier than us, had dispensed some wonderful advice: she told Mum that it was the correct etiquette never to replace the receiver before your caller does. We all had a good laugh at this because if both people were adhering to the same etiquette then they would both remain on the telephone until one of them expired.

Mum came into the lounge. 'It's Mr Walker for you, David.'

I was curious, but not alarmed. Tommy Walker, my manager, had never called me at home before, but I was sure there would be good reason. 'David, I have an urgent matter to discuss with you. Could I come over to see you now?'

'Of course,' I replied. I was alarmed now. Tommy had given no indication of what was so urgent that he was going to drive over to my parent's house late on a Sunday afternoon. I tried to think what I could have done wrong, but there was nothing. Was I going to be relieved of the captaincy? If so, he'd tell me at the ground. I sat back down in the armchair with a sense of trepidation.

When Tommy arrived, the family left us alone in the lounge. 'I'll get straight to the point, David. Tottenham Hotspur have been in contact and they have asked us whether we would agree to transfer you. Now, I'm sure you will have definite views on the matter and you must think hard about it. I am not asking you to go, because we think highly of you, as you well know, but you must consider the matter. I can tell you that Tottenham Hotspur are a forward-looking club and their manager, Bill Nicholson, is an honourable man. If you could call into my office at ten o'clock tomorrow and let me know your decision. Mr Nicholson is travelling up to Edinburgh tomorrow, too, and you will have the opportunity to meet him.'

Tommy rose and bid us all goodbye before driving off in his car. I was shell-shocked. We all were. Hearts were my life. I had honestly never seriously contemplated playing for anyone except Hearts, let alone a club in England. In the back of my mind, I envisaged that some day, maybe ten years hence, I'd have to retire and then I would join the backroom staff and work my way up to become manager. We turned over everything Tommy had said time and time again, but could not escape the conclusion that he wanted to sell me. If he didn't, he would have rejected Bill Nicholson's approach with no further ado. There was no obligation to present any transfer interest to the players then or now. He said it was my decision, yet he had invited Bill up the very next day to see me.

Having established that it was pretty self-evident that Hearts were willing and even wanted to sell me, we tried to work out why. I was young. I was captain. I was in good form. I enjoyed good relations with the manager and all the lads. I was captain of the national side. Hearts were doing well. Indeed, we were still in with a shout of retaining our League Championship. Did they need the money? I doubted it. Crowds were high. Not a lot of money had been spent in the transfer market. It was baffling.

Neither of our mums and dads liked the idea of Isobel and me and our young children moving down to London. I hadn't even moved on to such pragmatic thoughts. I was still struggling with the feeling of being rejected by Tommy Walker and Hearts. Isobel, as always, was the voice of reason.

'David, you talk to Mr Nicholson tomorrow. See how you feel then. The fact is that if Mr Walker and the club are of a mind to sell you, they will. If it means we have to move to London, then we will. We have to go where your work is. That's all there is to it.'

I didn't sleep well that Sunday night, but at least I started to gather my thoughts. If Tommy Walker had decided that I could or should go, then Tommy knew best. He had the interests of the club first, I was in no doubt of that, and he obviously felt this was right for Hearts. If it was right for Hearts, then it was right for me. It did occur to me to talk to Tommy and find out what his thinking really was, but if he wanted to tell me, he would have. This was a time when the boss knew best and we, the employees, did not demur. I wondered then if it was my foot. I had broken it three times now and it had kept me out of the team for some time on and off. Perhaps Tommy and others at the club felt that it was the beginning of a rocky road and that the foot was going to be the end of me. Maybe they had decided to lock in my value while they could. I couldn't imagine Tommy thinking in this way. He was a devout Christian and an honest man. There is no way he would have sold Bill Nicholson a dud knowingly. But he may have come under pressure from the directors or he may well have expressed the worry to Mr Nicholson and he had said he wanted to go ahead regardless. I'll never know now.

I read later that Bill Nicholson was actually trying to sign Mel Charles from Swansea when he alighted on me. Mel was the less famous brother of Welsh genius John Charles, but by all accounts he plumped to move to Arsenal rather than Tottenham. Some press reports said I was second on Bill's shopping list.

Mr Nicholson was in Tommy Walker's office when I knocked on his door at ten. Tommy introduced us and left us alone. I had heard of Bill, but knew little about him. He was only at the beginning of his managerial career and hadn't been the most famous of players. Not north of the border, anyway. He was thick-set with short, fair hair parted in the middle. His face looked like he might have boxed at one time. He seemed to me like a man from my father's generation or older, but thinking back now he was barely 40 years old.

'Dave, thank you for your time,' he began. 'I have always been a great admirer of you and have seen you play a number of times now. I think you could play an important part in my plans for Tottenham Hotspur. I cannot promise you cups and trophies, only time will tell, but I can promise you that we will always play exciting, entertaining and rewarding football.'

He went on to tell me that the club had money to make further acquisitions and assured me that I would always be on good wages. He couldn't top my current wage of £20 per week because that was the maximum but it went unsaid that sooner or later that would be abolished. He said I would be provided with a house, courtesy of the club, and that all my moving expenses would be paid for. In fact, the moving expenses being offered were more than generous.

I was impressed by Mr Nicholson's understatement, his modesty and his honesty. But I could also see that he was a determined man with a dream for his club and I accepted his terms there and then. If it was good enough for Danny Blanchflower, it was good enough for me. Bill said I could remain based in Edinburgh until the end of the season, but he would like me to travel down to Tottenham to meet the players at the earliest opportunity.

Tommy asked me to keep the news to myself until the paperwork had been completed. I learnt that the fee was to be £32,000, which was a record at the time for a defender or midfield player. This threw some more light on Hearts' decision to sell me: that money would go a long way in the Scottish transfer market. I resisted the temptation to speak to my teammates and on Tommy's advice drove straight home. Isobel took it all in her stride, but undoubtedly inside she was feeling the same as me: nervous, excited, sad.

The next day, I was told that everything had been tidied up and that I should take the train down to London and report to White Hart Lane. It was all very sudden. I was no longer a Heart of Midlothian player. Although I was enthused by the new challenges I faced in English football, I did feel bereaved. I was also uncomfortable with the indecent haste in which all of this was happening. I realised there was a transfer deadline to beat, but all the secrecy and my rapid despatch to London smacked of me having something to hide, which I did not. I would have liked to have said goodbye to my colleagues, I would have liked to have said goodbye to the fans, but that was not to be. In hindsight, I would have liked time to consider my options. It was just that, 48 hours earlier, I had not realised I was a man that needed to consider his options. For example, I believe that if Matt Busby knew that Hearts were prepared to let me go, he would have come in for me. I knew, trusted and admired Matt and, on paper, at that point in time, Manchester United were a far better bet than Spurs. The reality is that I would have gone to Old Trafford rather than White Hart Lane if I had had the choice. I'm glad now that I didn't, but that is what could have happened.

I packed my suitcase, donned my overcoat and set off for Waverley station. Isobel and the children would come down once a house had been found for us. In the meantime, I would return home between matches and continue to train with Hearts if I wished until the end of the season. I bought a newspaper from a kiosk and waited on the platform for the London train with a small bunch of friends and supporters who had got to hear about my departure. An elderly porter passed by and recognised me. Porters, for the benefit of readers under 30 years of age, were railway employees who helped passengers with their luggage. These were the days when the rail industry regarded passengers as customers rather than as a nuisance.

'Davie Mackay,' he greeted me, 'a pleasure to meet you.' He shook my hand warmly. 'Where are you off to then?'

'I'm down to London,' I said, 'I've signed for Tottenham Hotspur.' I could not see the point in keeping this whole business a secret and I suppose I really wanted to tell someone.

The porter pushed his trolley to one side and looked at me dumbfounded. He really was lost for words. My train pulled in and I boarded it. The porter stood motionless, staring. Finally, as I pulled down my window, he shook his head and said, 'Davie Mackay, the He'rts winnae be the same withoot you.'

CHAPTER SIX

When the Spurs

As Heart of Midlothian Football Club was born loosely from prisons and dancers, Tottenham Hotspur Football Club evolved from cricket and a historical English warrior immortalised by William Shakespeare. Back in the 1880s, Tottenham was, although well populated, a marshland area north of London, almost in rural Essex, and totally devoid of kebab shops. The railways had come earlier in the century and the working classes who made their living in the city were able to move away from the crush of central London and make homes in the new houses being put up adjacent to the railway lines. The area was an early commuter belt. Boys from two local schools – Tottenham Grammar and St John's Presbyterian School – had formed a cricket team they had called the Hotspur Cricket Club. They decided to add a football team to keep them occupied in winter when the cricket had dried up. They used local playing fields among the marshlands to play their cricket and football, and found they often had to defend these pitches from local ruffians who decided they were going to 'take' them. Whilst cricket was a long established sport in England, football was in its infancy and these boys were among thousands around the country that were taking up the sport and forming teams and leagues. They changed their football team's name to Tottenham Hotspur when they discovered another London side had also adopted the name 'Hotspur'.

No wonder it was a popular name. It smacks of buccaneering adventure. I never knew exactly what it meant, but I always liked the name. There was a picture comic in my youth called *Hotspur* and, if I remember rightly, it celebrated adventure, heroes and warriors from British history. The name certainly lifted Tottenham above the milieu of Uniteds, Citys and Rovers that ended up forming the Football League. Only recent entrant Rushden & Diamonds comes close in terms of inspirational club names.

Why those Middlesex schoolboys chose their title is not known. It may well have been something to do with the Percy family who at that time owned large swathes of land in the Tottenham area. Maybe it was one of their pitches the boys used. The Percy family had a famous ancestor – one Sir Henry Percy, who earned the moniker Harry Hotspur. Harry loved a fight and was renowned for wearing spurs in battle, hence his nickname. His family had remained loyal to King Richard II after he was toppled by his brother, who crowned himself King Henry IV. Young Harry, who was born at Alnwick Castle – currently famous for being the site used for the Harry Potter films – developed a thirst for battle and King Henry IV kept him occupied by sending him to quell rebellions all over England or to put down the marauding Welsh and Scots. These were handy diversions, as Henry knew that Harry had issues with him that would sooner or later rise to the surface.

And in 1403 they did. Harry Hotspur rounded up an army of rebels and set off to fight the Royal forces. The two armies met at Shrewsbury and an incredibly bloody battle was fought. Harry's men wore the emblem used by the Percys that depicted a white hart. Some 3,000 people were left dead, including Harry Hotspur himself. Just to make sure, King Henry had him hung, drawn and quartered, and ordered that various parts of his body be taken to major towns in England and shown to the people, so they would not be tempted to carry on rebelling. In that pre-television and newspaper age, how they would have known that these body parts actually belonged to Harry Hotspur and not the village drunk, I do not know. So that was Harry Hotspur. Was he a goodie or a baddie? It's not quite clear, but William Shakespeare certainly immortalised him by featuring him in two of his plays: *Richard II* and *Henry IV*.

Those Tottenham schoolboys turned to the vicar of Tottenham to help them develop and grow, and he found them a permanent home, away from the marshes, at a place called Dorset Villas, Northumberland Park. They played their first full season there, although they did cancel their last match to watch Blackburn Rovers beat Queens Park in the FA Cup final at the Oval. So entranced were they with Rovers, that they changed their strip for the following season to Blackburn's blue and white halves. They progressed steadily over the next few years, but were unable to secure membership of the Football League and it wasn't until 1895 that they finally turned professional. In 1896, after failing to get elected to the burgeoning Football League, they did succeed into getting voted into the First Division of the Southern League.

Things started to gather momentum from then on. The first manager, former Everton player Frank Brettell, was appointed and crowds of up to 14,000 were turning up at a new site in Northumberland Park. Records show that not all these supporters were particularly well behaved. In 1898, the ground was closed after fans assaulted three Luton Town players and another match against Woolwich Arsenal was abandoned due to the 'excessive use of bad language'. Just before the turn of the century, the club alighted on some nursery land behind the White Hart public house on Tottenham High Road. It was owned by Charringtons, the brewers, who had earmarked the site for cheap housing and whose occupants therefore would provide ready-made custom for their pubs. They agreed to allow the ground to be built, seeing a regular customer flow, and what is now known as White Hart Lane opened very quickly after negotiations were settled. Tottenham Hotspur are still there, as we know, and dominate the surroundings. Charringtons themselves, though, were swallowed up by Bass in the 1970s and Bass itself – a brand that was synonymous with British beer throughout my lifetime – has fallen down a corporate hole curiously called Six Continents.

In 1901, the year of the death of Queen Victoria, Spurs reached the FA Cup final and remarkably they were still a Southern League club. They were the last non-League club to do so. They played Sheffield United at Crystal Palace and a record 115,000 people crammed into the ground to watch the match. However, as surviving photographs clearly show, they could not have seen much. The terracing was barely tiered and the crush was such that the spectators encroached onto the pitch. During half-time, they meandered en masse out onto the turf to allow themselves and others breathing space. The match ended in a draw and was replayed at Bolton Wanderers' Burnden Park ground. Only 20,000 turned up for this one, chiefly because the Lancashire & Yorkshire Railway company refused to lay on cheap fares so there was little travelling support from London. Shame really because they missed Spurs' first FA Cup final victory after they outplayed Sheffield to win 3–1.

The FA Cup was already a big deal in the sporting calendar and the success would have leapfrogged Tottenham Hotspur into the national consciousness. However, it was not until 1908 that the club finally got out of the Southern League and into the more progressive and credible Football League. Even then, it was through the back door after Stoke City decided they could not survive in the Second Division on their then meagre attendances. The first League match was played on 1 September 1908 at White Hart Lane in front of 20,000 paying spectators: FA Cup holders Wolverhampton Wanderers were beaten 3–0. Tottenham's class propelled them to immediate promotion and by the summer of 1909, they were a First Division club.

Life in the First Division was tough, though, and Spurs struggled to hold their own and were eventually relegated just as the First World War broke out. The League was suspended shortly after hostilities began. In 1919–20, though, the team, strengthened by local winger Jimmy Dimmock, was resurgent and they stormed to the Second Division title. Dimmock is the first Spurs player I had heard of, as he scored in the FA Cup final the following year and also represented England. When I first arrived at White Hart Lane, there were still quite a few fans standing on the terraces who had watched him and that 1920s side. The FA Cup final of 1921, between Spurs and Wolves, was played at Chelsea's Stamford Bridge and Dimmock's goal was the only one of the game. Another well-known name and another Jimmy was also in that team: inside-forward Jimmy Seed, who was also held in high regard by older Tottenham fans (although there can be few left today who saw either men play). Seed was picked up from Sunderland after they decided he might not be able to continue his career after being gassed during the war. After giving Spurs some memorable years in the 1920s, he was let go to Sheffield Wednesday in 1927 and led them promptly to two League championships on the trot. Needless to say, his transfer was very unpopular with the fans. Seed went on to become a successful manager with Charlton Athletic in the 1930s and 1940s.

To rub further salt in the wounds, Tottenham had a particularly bad season in 1928 and were surprisingly relegated. The manager, Billy Minter, became the first but not the last Tottenham manager to resign through ill health, and Percy Smith, who had the task of slowly but carefully rebuilding an ageing team, replaced him. Some of the players that came through the ranks at that time were the beginning of a line and of a unique Spurs culture that still existed when I joined and that would drive them on to their finest hour. Cecil Poynton, who was trainer when I arrived, was already in the team and local boy Arthur Rowe was breaking through at centre-half. This younger side finally gained promotion back into the top flight in 1933 and the following season contested the Championship vigorously, finally finishing third behind Arsenal and Huddersfield, two great sides touched by the genius of Herbert Chapman. However, the side inexplicably ran out of steam again in 1934–35 and were relegated once more.

Percy Smith resigned as manager and was replaced by Jack Tresadern, whose place in footballing history is assured for captaining West Ham in the first Wembley FA Cup final in 1923

– the final now famously remembered as the 'White Horse Final' because a solitary policeman on a white horse managed to clear the massive crowd that had spilled onto the pitch. Arthur Rowe was by then captain, but the side remained middling in the Second Division, although they did enjoy a number of good FA Cup runs. In desperation, the board looked to the man who had managed them between 1913 and 1927, their best years thus far, the dispute they had had over money now forgotten in the sands of time. Peter McWilliam replaced Jack Tresadern in 1938. By this time, a boy from Scarborough had made his debut. His father ran a horse transport service in the Yorkshire seaside town and Spurs scouts had offered the boy terms and he was soon playing for the nursery club Northfleet. His name was Bill Nicholson.

The Second World War put paid to any immediate revival at Spurs, as the structured professional football game was again suspended. However, younger players such as Nicholson, goalkeeper Ted Ditchburn, Ron Burgess and Les Medley kept their hand in and developed as good footballers throughout wartime football. In 1945 when the war ended, Peter McWilliam decided he was too old to continue in management and Joe Hulme, a member of the legendary Herbert Chapman Arsenal side of the 1930s, replaced him. Hulme did not manage to get Tottenham out of the Second Division but, during his three years in charge, he gelled the team together and started the ball rolling with the signing of one Alfred Ramsey, a promising right-back from Southampton. He also took the club to the semi-finals of the FA Cup in 1948, where they succumbed only to Stanley Matthews and his Blackpool side.

Hulme was ousted in favour of Arthur Rowe, who, since retiring from playing for Spurs in 1939, had been coaching in Hungary and more recently transforming non-League Chelmsford City into an exciting, slick outfit. His outlook was described as 'progressive' and, being one of the few English managers who had worked abroad at that time, his mind was very open to new ideas. The style of play in Britain had hardly changed at all in the first 50 or 60 years of professional football. Centre-forwards were big strapping men to be found with crosses from the two wingers who would have dribbled past the full-backs who had been marking them religiously. Centre-halves were even bigger and their job was to stop attacks: to clear the ball whether with head or with feet. Positions were pretty much fixed and most players would not stray far from their allotted few square feet of turf. Arthur Rowe had a vision of something quite different. He had an idea of how to play, transmitted it to his squad and took English football by storm.

It was called 'push and run' and now seems an astonishingly simple footballing philosophy, but at the time it was new and took all the other clubs completely by surprise. Arthur's slogan was 'make it simple – make it quick'. He believed that keeping possession of the ball was all-important and that only fast, short and accurate passing could do this effectively and consistently: *pushing* the ball and then *running* into space. Arthur did not change the line-up (other than the eventual signing of Alf Ramsey) that Joe Hulme had used to finish consistently in the top half of the Second Division over the previous few years, but he did change the way they played almost immediately. In 1949–50, they stormed through the season and finished as Second Division champions despite only taking a solitary point from their final five games. Opposing teams could not cope with the style of play and most were left floundering as the likes of Bill Nicholson, Alf Ramsey, Eddie Bailey (who would become Bill's right-hand man during his tenure as manager of Spurs), Len Duquemin and the rest spread the ball around like they had some divine right to it. They managed to bang in 80-odd goals whilst conceding 35 at the other end, but most importantly it was exciting, breathtaking and beautiful football. The crowd loved it and could never forget it. It is from this period of the early 1950s that Tottenham's pedigree as a side that plays entertaining football was really established and that goal has underpinned the ethos at the club ever since. It is a fact that at Spurs they would rather lose a trophy and play well than win a trophy and play badly. Or at least it was in my time and beyond.

Back in the First Division at last, Spurs were not considered a great threat and certainly not contenders to become League champions. Push and run, experts decided, would not work in the top flight, therefore no plans were made to deal with Tottenham's tactics or maybe, heaven forbid, even adopt them. How wrong everyone was. It took them a few games to find their feet, but at the end of September they embarked on a winning streak of eight games in which they scored an incredible twenty-eight goals. These matches included a 7–0 drubbing of Jackie Milburn's Newcastle United, the club that would win the FA Cup that season and the following one. Suddenly, everyone was taking notice and the turnstiles clicked at White Hart Lane like they never had before and never have since – 70,000 jammed into that Newcastle fixture alone.

With only Manchester United close, Tottenham Hotspur became League champions in 1950–51 for the first time in their history. It was an incredible feat to come from the Second Division to best team in the country in two seasons. Even more incredible was that the team contained no superstars and no regular international players other than Alf Ramsey. This really was a team in the pure sense of the word. Interestingly, Alf Ramsey himself would emulate this feat a decade later when, as manager of Ipswich Town, he took them from Second Division to League champions in successive seasons with players whose names were largely unknown outside of East Anglia. Tottenham were the toast of the country. Push and run was the talk of bar rooms and had England had a full-time international team manager and not a selection committee, Arthur Rowe would surely have been offered the post.

The momentum continued into the following season, although, at the death, Manchester United managed to turn the tables and pipped Spurs for the Championship by four points. Ted Ditchburn, the goalkeeper, and Eddie Bailey had joined Ramsey in the England team and deservedly the quiet but determined Bill Nicholson also got a call-up. It was tougher in 1952–53: the combination of the side beginning to age (Bill Nicholson was 34 and Alf Ramsey 32) and other teams learning how to deal with the quick passing style of play took the edge off Tottenham's form. They still finished tenth and were only knocked out of the FA Cup at the semi-final stage by the famous Stanley Matthews–Stanley Mortensen Blackpool side (again) that would win it in such style in the now legendary 'Matthews Cup Final' of 1953.

Shortly after, the decline accelerated and in the next two seasons relegation was avoided only by a hair's breadth. Arthur Rowe came in for much criticism for not replacing and replenishing his ageing squad. In 1955–56, when Tottenham only avoided the Second Division by one place, nine of the squad had played in the League Championship season of 1950–51. It was a sad fizzing out of a firework team that had glowed and sprayed so brightly. Rowe took it all very personally and the strain affected his health. Following a nervous breakdown, he sadly resigned. Arthur Rowe should never have reproached himself: not only did he devote his life to Spurs and leave them with a proud history, he also left them with their future. In December 1954, shortly before he fell ill, he signed one Daniel Blanchflower from Aston Villa Football Club.

Danny and Arthur were destined to come together. It was a shame that their union came just a smidgeon too late for Arthur Rowe. Like Arthur, Danny was a deep thinker, a visionary for whom football was not just a job but a vocation. Born in industrial Belfast, he started his career with Glentoran: like me with Hearts, this was his boyhood dream come true. But he became frustrated with his club's lack of ambition and commitment to the future (also, if truth be told, the limited stage they played on) and at the age of 22 he moved into English football with Second Division Barnsley. His intelligent, crafted and superior football became the talk of Oakwell. As Barnsley's only supporter with a national voice, Michael Parkinson's word is all we have for this. Northern Ireland, who were never spoilt for world-class footballers, soon picked up on him and in 1949 an international career that stretched into the next two decades began. As documented earlier, that international career reached its peak when Blanchflower as captain and Peter Doherty as manager shocked and delighted everyone at the 1958 World Cup finals in Sweden with exquisite football and a brave showing.

Danny's frustrations came to the fore again at Barnsley. He

couldn't keep his mouth shut, which in the forelock-tugging '50s was as good as asking for your cards. He railed against mediocrity and even Parky might acknowledge that that was not in short supply at Oakwell at the time. Danny particularly detested having his and his club's destiny controlled by directors who knew nothing about the game. His game. It incensed him that affluent men, whose only qualification was that they owned three butcher shops in town, could influence team selection. When Oakwell finally became too small for both Barnsley FC and Danny Blanchflower, he was transferred to Aston Villa.

Villa were a big club with an illustrious history and, being in the First Division, provided Danny with the theatre he craved and deserved. He soon became a big fish around the Midlands and began broadcasting on radio and writing his own newspaper columns. Many leading players wrote columns for newspapers or football magazines at the time, but I imagine that Danny's was the first not to be ghosted in any way. Few journalists could have matched his powers of analysis, wit and insight in any case. Inevitably, at a time when footballers were starting to rebel against unfair contracts and conditions, Danny did not hold back and he fell into dispute with the management at Villa Park. He made them feel under threat. They loved a good footballer – there was no doubt that Danny soon established himself as the linchpin of their improving side – and they would even accept a footballer that was intelligent, but dealing with one that was articulate and had a platform to voice his opinions was a bridge too far.

So it was, then, halfway through the 1954–55 season that he moved to Tottenham Hotspur, to possibly the only manager he could have played under for any sustained period. Danny would have observed push and run from a distance and would have delighted in Arthur Rowe's success in upsetting the status quo and revelled in the wonderful football that had been played. He would also have understood the predicament Arthur was in: having to break up a side very dear to him. I am sure the two men discussed in detail where they would go next and how they could fashion the second great Spurs side of the 1950s.

He made a quick impact, as Spurs' performance post-Christmas was appreciably better than the first half of the season and the club avoided relegation by finishing 16th. At one point, it had looked inevitable. But before Danny and Arthur could take stock and build on their ideas and dreams, Arthur fell ill and was replaced by Jimmy Anderson, a backroom member of staff who had, incredibly, been working at Tottenham since 1908. He would have rubbed shoulders with some of the very boys that had started the club 20 years earlier. Needless to say, this was a development that did not sit well with Danny, and he and Jimmy Anderson did not see eye to eye. Jimmy saw Danny as a threat and Danny saw Jimmy as a rudderless stop-gap. At one point, Jimmy stripped Danny of the captaincy and it looked like the principled but argumentative Irishman could be on his way again.

But Danny was pragmatic. He knew that Anderson was getting on and that former player Bill Nicholson, now the assistant manager, was being groomed for the job. He also knew that, despite the season almost ending in relegation, the second half of the season had been much better than the first. They had reached the semi-finals of the FA Cup. Also Tony Marchi had broken into the first team and a big centre-forward named Bobby Smith had arrived from Chelsea. There were the beginnings of a good new side forming.

The 1956–57 season proved that Danny's hunches were correct. Against all odds, they finished runners-up to Matt Busby's all-conquering and tragically doomed young Manchester United side. Bobby Smith, Tony Marchi and little Tommy Harmer found the net 45 times between them. However, getting knocked out of the FA Cup by Third Division Bournemouth gave momentum to the notion that Tottenham were still a side in decline. Friction also remained between Jimmy Anderson and his captain. Danny was accustomed to taking control once the players were out on the pitch and Anderson resented this. Sometimes Danny would even alter formations and tactics during the game and understandably this led to public arguments. Once when Jimmy dropped him in an effort to assert his authority, Danny's friends on the press had ensured it was plastered all over the back pages. The same happened when he was relieved of his captaincy.

To Jimmy's credit, he knew that he did not have the luxury of keeping a man of Danny's calibre out of the team and because of this, although they had a relationship based on brinkmanship, he stopped short of allowing things to come to a final head.

The 1957–58 season was also a good one by anybody's standards, with the club finishing in third position. Stan Cullis's Wolverhampton Wanderers, captained by Billy Wright, were the deserved champions. Billy was the David Beckham of his day: captaining England, marrying a pop star (one of the Beverley Sisters) and his image being used as a marketing tool for various consumer products. It said something about Danny Blanchflower's rising stock in the game that it was he and not Billy that picked up the Football Writers' Association Footballer of the Year award that season. Manager Jimmy Anderson had also laid some valuable foundations by signing Cliff Jones, the talented winger I had played against in the army, from Swansea and his earlier signings Terry Medwin and Terry Dyson were clicking into gear. Bobby Smith excelled himself up front with 36 goals.

Yet 1958–59 could not have got off to a poorer start, with twelve goals conceded and consecutive defeats in the first three matches. Jimmy Anderson felt the pressure and in October (with Tottenham lying in 16th place), he tendered his resignation, citing ill health. Bill Nicholson was installed seamlessly as the new manager. His first game was at home to Everton, and Spurs rampaged to a 10–4 victory. Bobby Smith grabbed four of the goals. He quipped to Bill after the game: 'Can't guarantee this every week, boss.'

Bobby's tongue-in-cheek remark was to prove more accurate than he could have predicted; although the next game was won 4–3 against Leicester, Spurs only managed to win once in the next 11 matches. Relegation loomed. In desperation, Bill dropped Danny Blanchflower. Bill complained that Danny's compulsion to go forward was jeopardising the defence and this was part of the reason Tottenham were leaking goals. Danny interpreted this as him not playing a part in Bill's long-term plans. After all, he was 33 years of age by then. He went to see the manager and requested a transfer and Bill promptly turned him down. He just wanted Danny to see things his way. There was a battle to win; the battle for survival in Division One. Extreme measures were called for, even if this meant checking one's natural playing instincts. In February, with a new understanding between manager and captain, Danny Blanchflower was restored to the first team. Meanwhile, Cliff Jones was back in the team after being quickly put out with a hairline fracture. He was starting to look good.

On Wednesday, 18 March 1959, I stepped out of Manor Park Tube station into the daylight, having travelled from my hotel in St Pancras. I waited outside for the bus as I had been told to and, sure enough, one soon came along. I pulled myself on by the pole and went straight upstairs. A bus conductor followed me up the curling steps, his silver ticket vending machine hanging around his neck, a Capstan cigarette stuck to his lower lip.

'Where to, cocker?'

'White Hart Lane, please.'

CHAPTER SEVEN

The Jigsaw

My first impression of White Hart Lane was its enormity. Everything from the toilets to the main stand was bigger than the set-up at Tynecastle. The pitch appeared larger. Even the players seemed to tower over me. Bill Nicholson took me around the place and introduced me to all the staff. I chatted briefly to Cecil Poynton, the trainer, about my foot injury and he made reassuring noises about knocking it into shape. One by one, I met the players, who were all very welcoming and nice to me. A few months earlier, I had played against them in a friendly at Hibernian. Every year, a team of Hibs and Hearts players would play a friendly against a big-name club in a showcase of the best of Edinburgh football and Spurs had been the last opponents. They walloped us 3–1 and were clearly a superior side, but if it had not been for that match, with a couple of exceptions, I would have barely heard of any of these men.

Bobby Smith, Ted Ditchburn, Mel Hopkins and Maurice Norman were among the formidably framed men. Ted had been around for years and was in the final weeks of his Tottenham career. He had kept goal in the push-and-run side, and was part of the woodwork and held in great esteem. I was surprised to learn that he and Bill Nicholson lived in club houses adjacent to each other just outside the ground. Little Tommy Harmer, whose Tottenham career was destined to fall between the push-and-run and Double-winning teams, was particularly chatty. Although we did not play in the same team for very long, I grew to really like and admire this little scamp of a goal poacher. He was a crowd favourite who knew how to entertain, yet football history has not remembered him in the same way as many lesser players. Danny Blanchflower greeted me warmly and immediately worked his Irish charm to the full.

'Don't be overawed,' he grinned, 'you're a great player. One of the best I've played against. I've been telling Bill Nick as much for a while now. You're in good company here, Dave. This is a good side and getting better by the day. Relegation? My foot!'

He was referring to Tottenham's precarious position near the floor of the First Division. I hadn't really considered that there was a real possibility I could soon be playing English Second Division football, but I should have – the club had lost nine of the previous fifteen League games before my arrival.

I made my debut a few days later on Saturday, 21 March 1959, at home to Manchester City. Cecil Poynton had strapped my foot up good and I did not let on how much it was paining me; the adrenalin of the occasion saw me through. The Prime Minister at the time was Harold Macmillan and he had recently declared that Britain had never had it so good. In my case, he was right. Lonnie Donegan, known for singing cockney songs, was asking whether our chewing gum lost its flavour on our bedposts overnight and we all laughed. London had been enveloped in fog and smog the like of which we no longer see since people stopped using coal to heat their homes. The 34,000 crowd gave me a rousing reception even though they would not have known me and had never seen me play. Thankfully, I did not let them down and played a good game in a decisive 3–1 victory. Our goals came from Terry Medwin, Bobby Smith and a penalty from Cliff Jones.

Debuts are so crucial. Because a player can be so tense, it's likely he will perform worse than normal. If he has a bad game, the crowd are unimpressed and can become hostile. The player becomes more pressurised and his game suffers. A vicious circle develops that is hard to break. I know of players that have never been able to settle at a club because of this cycle, yet they have gone elsewhere and excelled. I was lucky: in the opening seconds, I hit a shot that soared only just over the bar and had goalkeeper Bert Trautmann beaten. Later in the game, Terry Medwin scored from my pass. It was a good performance even though the pace of the game was significantly faster than that to which I was accustomed. I realised that I would have to train much harder and more often. I was particularly pleased with how Danny Blanchflower and I struck up an immediate understanding. We both loved to go forward and in that initial game (and thereafter) we did this, with the other slipping behind to cover lest any gaps opened up in the defence.

I devoured the London national papers on the Sunday morning in my hotel. Alan Hoby in the *Sunday Express* wrote: 'Mackay steadied the entire defence. There was a new poise and confidence about Spurs' suspect back division which stemmed from Mackay's relish for English First Division football.'

Frank Butler, another respected writer, went further in the *News of the World*: 'Mackay played an important and calculated part in this victory, which almost certainly guarantees Spurs First Division football next season. I expect to see the Scot develop into a first-class skipper for Spurs in the years to come.'

Frank was right. We won the following week at Villa Park and lost only twice in the last nine games. Although we managed to finish only in 18th position, after the Aston Villa game, we were practically safe. I was out for some of those final matches and did not play on the losing side at Tottenham until October 1959 – well into the following season.

It was not my foot that kept me out for some of those matches at the close of 1958–59, but a boil. You never hear of them these days. Thank God. Those obscene puss-filled mega-pimples that seemed to afflict young men. I never hear of women getting them, but then I wouldn't, would I? It must have been something in the water. Today, it would be called an abscess. Just in the same way as nobody has headaches any more – they have a migraine. Nobody has stomach upsets – they have food poisoning. And nobody has the blues – they are suffering from depression and stress. And, of course, the common cold has been replaced by flu or even pneumonia. It is no longer enough for us as a society to just be stricken with the common ailments.

Back home, there was great consternation about my transfer to Spurs. Fans were up in arms and the papers were full of it. Most people, like myself, could not understand the logic of selling me at a time when the Championship was still within grasp and they felt that my sale was tantamount to surrendering to Rangers. Sadly, that was to happen and Hearts ended the season as close runners-up to the Glasgow club. Fortunately for my peace of mind, nobody attached any blame to me, even though one newspaper carried a story quoting me as saying that if I had not been transferred, I would have asked for one anyway, and that it was my aim to play in England. That was my first experience of journalists simply making things up. I could not believe that they could get away with it. The chap in question probably thought that, now I lived in London, I would never read the article. The wrath of the fans was short-lived, and they and I were delighted that Hearts nicked the Championship back (for a fourth time) in 1959–60, as well as the League Cup. Tommy Walker had successfully moulded a second great side without the likes of the Terrible Trio or me, but oddly he then sold Alex Young and George Thomson, arguably the club's two best players, to Everton. The 1960s, although there were a few high spots, became largely a decade of decline at Tynecastle.

My family were eager to hear about life at Tottenham and in London. I think they imagined that I was mixing with the in-crowd and enjoying the bright lights. The reality was that I had done little more than travel up and down Tottenham High Road. My brothers were all out of professional football by then, but they continued to follow and support my career enthusiastically. Frank had been for a trial with Manchester United in 1956, and had been asked back, but for reasons best known to himself he never returned. During his National Service, he played with Bobby Charlton and Duncan Edwards for the army and in 1957 Everton signed him. When he did not break through at Goodison Park, he returned to Scotland and signed for Alloa Athletic but a knee injury ended his career in 1959.

I played for Scotland against England at Wembley before the season ended and we lost to a single Bobby Charlton goal. Tommy Docherty was in the team and he congratulated me on my move to Tottenham.

'Where are you living?' he asked. I told him about the hotel and how Isobel was coming down when she could to look at houses.

'We can't have you living in a bloody hotel. You're moving in with my wife and me and I won't hear of anything else.'

And so I moved to Cockfosters as Tommy and Agnes Docherty's lodger. They were very kind to a new boy in town and looked after me well. Tommy was obsessed with football, even more than me, and little else was discussed in that household. I can see him now at the dinner table getting agitated about some player, manager or official, only stopping his stream of invective when Agnes quietly put his dinner down in front of him. He'd be silent as he ate and then seconds after the final mouthful had slipped down his gullet, he'd start back up where he had left off. Who said he only started doing after-dinner speeches when his career in football ended?

On Sundays, his day off, he'd be up early and off to a charity match. He regularly refereed for the Showbiz Eleven and he'd drag me along to run the line. He lived and breathed football, and I knew even then that he would go into football management, which he did, and that he would rub up the establishment along the way, which he did. Tommy was not a rebel or a troublemaker, as he has sometimes been portrayed. He was merely passionate and knowledgeable, and they were two qualities that the men who ran the game at that time lacked the most.

Tottenham Hotspur had suggested to Isobel and me that we could look to rent a house that would be valued at around £4,000. We eventually found a place in Southgate and Isobel and the children finally moved down. Isobel is a determined woman and she took the whole upheaval in her stride, but one afternoon when I arrived home I found her sobbing in the lounge. I'd been gone since the Friday, having been to an away match, and Isobel's mum and brother Tom had also just left for home and she had felt alone for the first time. She had been to the local shops and had queued in the butcher shop for a Sunday joint. When it came to her turn she asked for what she wanted, but the butcher could not understand what she was saying. Or said he couldn't.

Both our accents would have been stronger then than they are now and Scottish accents were rarely encountered in London. The only time they were heard even on the television was when Kenneth McKellar sang in his obligatory kilt on New Year's Eve. Around this time, a song called 'A Scottish Soldier' by Andy Stewart was in the charts and in England this seemed to have great novelty value. Shortly after, a programme called *Dr Finlay's Casebook* became popular on TV, and Janet, the doctor's assistant, played by Barbara Mullen, who had a strong Scottish brogue, became the most mimicked person in England for a while, such was the novelty of a Scottish accent in the south of England.

I happened to mention it in training the next day. Danny Blanchflower laughed. He said that when he first arrived in London, people expressed surprise that he was not wearing a donkey jacket and digging up the roads. When I got home that afternoon, Isobel was in much higher spirits.

'I had a caller today,' she told me.

It transpired that a lady had knocked on the door and introduced herself as Betty Blanchflower, Danny's wife, and had taken her back to her house for coffee. Isobel started to settle from then on, and she and Betty became great friends.

We both continued to have problems making ourselves understood, but after a few weeks could see the funny side of it. In Scotland, we say 'half loaf' for a loaf. This one is not the fault of the English and I stopped using it the first time I visited the baker's and the man brandished a loaf at me and said, 'So you want me to cut this in half then, mate?'

When we first joined the other players and their wives for

drinks at a Spurs supporters' dance, John Hempstead, a Scottish friend of ours, asked Isobel what she would like to drink and she ordered a vodka and Coke. She almost passed out when she sipped the drink.

'John, I don't know what this is, but it's not vodka and Coke,' she whispered.

John queried it with the barman.

'I thought that was an unusual drink,' he explained. 'I assumed that you Scots must drink vodka and port.'

We took the new house – 26 Whitehouse Way – from a celebrity named Terry Hall. He was a ventriloquist and was on the TV a good deal with his puppet Lenny the Lion. I guess he was on the up and moving on to a bigger place. As we explored the nooks and crannies, I found a crumpled Lenny lying in the cupboard, forlorn with its mane all tatty.

'Isobel, you best call the estate agents. Terry Hall has left Lenny here. He'll be worried.'

'Don't be so stupid, David. He'll have lots of Lennys. This is obviously an old discarded one.'

I visibly deflated. It registered for the first time that the puppets were not real. That Harry Corbett probably had a dozen Sootys and Ray Allen a trunk full of Lord Charleses. It was one of those finding-out-Father-Christmas-is-not-real moments. Terry and Lenny did go on to bigger things and I even recall The Beatles appearing on their show in the early 1960s, although I have no idea where they are now. Lenny and Terry, that is, not The Beatles. The last time I recall seeing Lenny was on the commercial channels proclaiming that Trebor Mints were a minty bit stronger.

Just as the season ended, I was picked again to play for Scotland against West Germany in a friendly at Hampden Park. Germany were a good side and getting better, and it was to our credit that we prevailed by three goals to two. One of their strikes came from their great forward, Uwe Seeler, who seven years later would enter English history books as captain of the national side that lost in the World Cup final to Bobby Moore and the boys. However, the player that really impressed me was our own John

White. A young inside-forward with Falkirk, he was making his international debut and played a great intuitive game and also managed to get on the score sheet. He came from Musselburgh, near to Isobel's village, and had started out with Alloa Athletic before Falkirk snapped him up. Over the previous months, he had been making real waves in Scottish football. I made a mental note to tell Bill Nicholson about him, as Bill had more than once asked me about any up and coming talent in Scotland that I could recommend.

Just before we moved to Southgate and almost immediately after the West Germany game, I was off to Russia on tour. I had visited South Africa with Hearts and my experience of foreign lands was limited to that one trip. Communist Russia was a very different scenario. It was colder for a start and the surroundings were far more austere than white Cape Town or Johannesburg. But, again, our hosts were adept at steering us clear of anything that might disturb us in any way. We did all the touristy things when we weren't playing football: we visited Red Square, saw Lenin lying in state and watched the Moscow State Circus. Four times. It was some circus, though. At home, I'd visited the Bertram Mills' Circus with Coco the Clown and curiosities like boxing kangaroos, but Moscow was Hollywood compared with Bertram Mills' Pinewood. Most importantly, though, as a group of men we bonded together and I am sure that trip accelerated the team spirit, understanding and telepathy that developed between us as players and as friends. I roomed with Cliff Jones and we got on like a house on fire, probably because he is Welsh and I am Scottish, and neither of us understood a word the other said. We had some good results too, beating Torpedo Moscow and Dynamo Kiev.

On our return, Bill Nicholson visited Scotland again to buy the Dundee and Scottish international goalkeeper Bill Brown. I had played with Bill for Scotland and against him at Hearts, and rated him very highly. Our other goalkeepers were Ted Ditchburn, who was a veteran of the push-and-run side, and Ron Reynolds, who had lost the top of his finger in an accident. This left just John Hollowbread, who had played well for Spurs, but Bill felt he needed another keeper. Bill Brown proved to be an integral part of the side that was quickly forming.

Tours, internationals and friendly matches over, I was keen to resume training before the 1959–60 season opened. I had never been more excited about a new season. I loved the English game and just knew that at Spurs we had something special coming together. Our 18th-place finish was a reflection of early-season turbulence rather than our potential. My respect for Bill Nicholson and his team grew daily. The assistant manager, Harold Evans, was a wonderful man and, like Bill, had very forward-looking ideas. He drafted in a famous weightlifter of the time, Bill Watson, and in short but effective sessions he built us up physically. Each morning, we focused on something different, whether it was ball work, running or set pieces. On Fridays, we were allowed to do what we wanted. Not go off to the pub or golf course, but to decide which element of the training programme we felt we needed to work on the most. It was an enlightening regime.

I relished the five-a-side games more than anything, especially when we had our gymnasium built and we were enclosed. When there was no way out. I truly believe that five-a-side is the best training method. It builds team spirit, you learn about each other and it makes you fit. From the first day, I took no prisoners and fights would occasionally break out. I'd love to get one of my colleagues with the ball in the corner and not allow him out. Sometimes this would lead to an elbow in the guts or tempers fraying, but once it was over, it was over. Nobody bore any grudges.

Before the gym was built, we sometimes played five-a-side matches on the concrete outside the stadium and I can recall, not long after I had joined, indulging in my first game and playing as if it was for real. I knew no different. Ron Henry had the ball and I chased him and committed to a long sliding tackle. Very stupid on tarmac. The burn mark on my leg came up immediately. Ron looked down at me, shaking his head and saying, 'Are you f*****g mad?'

The season could barely have got off to a better start after we stormed Newcastle at St James's Park and won 5–1. Cliff Jones bagged a hat-trick. Good results followed and in the September, we visited Matt Busby's Manchester United and inflicted the same result on them. In this match, I scored my first goal for Spurs. The following week I was able to do it again for the home crowd in yet another 5–1 win, this time over Preston North End. I loved pushing forward like Danny Blanchflower and he was generous in allowing me to do so and covering for me. I ended the season having scored 11 goals, with only Cliff Jones and Bobby Smith managing more. Danny and I were playing gloriously together, even if I say so myself. The newspapers started to rave about Spurs generally – predicting great things. They said I had brought a steel-like quality to the side and that my presence had enabled Danny to flower even more than he had already. One reporter commented: 'Danny Blanchflower is telepathic and Dave Mackay is psychopathic.'

I wasn't too sure about how to take that, but it was the beginning of a myth that was starting to build around my tackling and so-called toughness.

We didn't lose until October and our unlucky 13th League game. Our opponents were Sheffield Wednesday, who became our bogey side. They were fresh up from the Second Division and were packed with large, uncompromising Yorkshiremen. Many teams, including ourselves, found it hard to play against the likes of Gerry Young, Don Megson, John Fantham and Peter Swan but, all credit to them, they held their own in the top flight, often finishing up high and, in 1966, making the FA Cup final.

Sadly, Peter Swan and his colleague David 'Bronco' Layne were later convicted in a match-fixing scandal exposed by a Sunday newspaper and they, with others, were sent to prison and were effectively out of the game. It was sad because they were good players with good careers ahead of them, but I had and still have no sympathy for them. This was my game, remember, and that of millions of others – the game we loved and around which our lives would always revolve. They stained it and I still cannot understand why. Syndicates were apparently betting on the outcomes of games and these footballers were allegedly throwing matches. I can't see it. You'd need at least three players on a side, more likely five, to be able to achieve this for a start. I could see the temptation for some, though. The football pools didn't help. Sometimes I picked up the coupon and saw that Hearts, for example, were 50–1 to lose 4–0 at home. If you had an utterly corrupt bunch of players it could be tempting to raise £50 a piece and back this result and then try and engineer it – £2,500 in the 1950s would have been life-changing for young men on £20 per week. It has been claimed by a number of ex-footballers since that the Swan match-fixing case was not an isolated incident and that corruption was widespread. I can honestly say that I never experienced this at all nor do I know of any of my colleagues who did either. It may be because people guessed that if they approached me with such a proposition, they would have been punched squarely on the jaw.

That Wednesday defeat was significant for another reason. Bill Nicholson had been on a raiding mission across the border and had returned with John White, not exactly kicking and screaming, under his arm. Danny and I were delighted. We knew just how good he was. Although we lost that day, he managed to score our only goal on this, his debut, and impress his other teammates. John was a great player who shared Danny's ability to find space and could read the game better than most forwards of the day. Years later, they called Martin Peters 'The Ghost' at both Upton Park and White Hart Lane. Well, John had the nickname first for literally ghosting into space. Although he scored goals, he was generous and thoughtful and made many, many more for others. He was the final piece of the jigsaw. No doubt about it.

We became great friends and I warmed to his modesty and his quiet sense of humour. He was passionate about the game, like me, and very often he and I would return to training after dinner when the other lads had gone off home and practise further. Even when I went, he'd stay and continue running, running and running. I would not say he was the fittest player at White Hart Lane, but he was the hardest trainer. Not that he was obsessed.

John loved to come for a drink with the lads, too, and would entertain us with his off-the-wall antics. He'd be sitting next to a stranger in the pub and would just rest his head on their shoulder as the other man shuffled along the seat warily; or take a chrysanthemum from a vase and casually eat it. He'd probably been watching *Candid Camera*.

John moved in with Harry Evans, the assistant manager, who also lived near the ground in the Tottenham Hotspur community, and he soon fell in love with Harry's daughter Sandra. They were later married and a happier couple you could not meet. Tottenham really was a tight-knit community club in those days. For example, Bill Nicholson's wife Grace, known to us all as Darkie on account of her dark-coloured hair, was often seen around the vicinity. 'Hello, Darkie,' we'd shout with a wave. Today we'd be risking life and limb saying something like that across the north London streets.

The season continued at a furious pace and we were up there with the leaders throughout. In January 1960, we were drawn against lowly Crewe Alexandra in the FA Cup and were nearly upset when they held us gallantly 2–2 at Gresty Road in front of a record 20,000 people. In the replay, we weren't taking any chances and destroyed them by 13–2, a record win for Spurs in senior football. Five of our goals were scored by Les Allen, a bustling forward we had signed from Chelsea. A generation later, Les's son Clive would also make a big name for himself at Spurs and in football generally. I remember the game not only for the fancy scoreline but also because Bill Nicholson gave me a bollocking afterwards.

'Dave, I don't expect to see you going in on tackles like that, risking injury to yourself and others, and getting booked or sent off. Anyone would have thought we were ten goals behind not ten goals up.' He had a point.

I was only trying to repay Bill's kindness by showing my commitment. He had told me I could set off straight away after the game for a couple of days to see Isobel in Scotland, where she was about to give birth in an Edinburgh hospital to our third child. Even though we were now living in London, we wanted any children to be born in Scotland so they could play football for their country when they grew up, should they be that way inclined. When I got there Isobel said, 'Our baby won't be playing for Scotland, David.'

'Why not?' I asked, just a little concerned.

'Because he's a girl called Valerie.'

CHAPTER EIGHT

The Double Bubble

History has it that before we embarked on the 1960–61 season Danny Blanchflower told Fred Wale and the other directors at Tottenham that we would win the League and FA Cup Double. He is also meant to have rallied the players and said much the same thing. I don't remember this at all, but that is not to say he did not say it. Danny came out with things like this all the time. It was all part of him building the rest of us up and therefore it would not have stuck in my mind. He also said we'd go through the season and win every game; I remember that because for a while it looked like we would. Doing the Double would have appealed to Danny because no team had managed it in the twentieth century (although some had got close) and achieving it would cement his place in history. Even he would have accepted that captaining Northern Ireland to a World Cup victory was a non-runner. In his view, captaining a Double-winning team was the next best thing.

Before we gathered for the new season, I had some international duty to attend to. At the close of the last season, Bill Brown, John White and I had been disappointed by Bill Nicholson's decision not to allow us leave to play for Scotland against England at Hampden Park. I had played England at Wembley, but never in front of my home crowd. It is something I desperately wanted to do, but Bill was adamant, saying that we had to put our club before our country and that it was a crucial time in the season. It was, but as there were three of us we felt it was bit unfair on Scotland – but then Bill was English. We did not argue – footballers generally didn't then – but we were in a huff and probably not in the best frame of mind for the upcoming League match. There were no winners really. Scotland only managed a 1–1 draw and Spurs suffered a rare defeat against Everton.

I was free to join the Scottish side for a tour of Europe in the close season, though. We weren't particularly successful, losing to Poland at Hampden, then in Austria and Turkey, but managing a draw with Hungary. After the Turkey game, we were asked to attend an official function in Ankara and we all sat down to dinner on a long banqueting table dressed in our international blazers. The Turkish players were opposite and the top brass, their equivalent of the Football Association, I guess, sat at the top table. Because of the language barrier, players mainly talked and drank amongst themselves. We were in a mischievous mood and Denis Law decided to make me a dare. Denis knew me well and made sure there was some money involved.

'Right,' said Denis, 'you've got to take your shoes and socks off and walk the length of this table.' I sized up the situation. I was a tad worried that I might cause offence because I had read somewhere that in Arabian culture it is impolite to show the soles of one's feet. However, it wasn't the soles of my feet that would be on view. And ten pounds is ten pounds. I whipped off my footwear, jumped onto the table and strolled up to the end, dodging the condiments on the way. All eyes were soon on me. I jumped down in front of the Turkish officials.

'Please forgive me, but in Scotland it is an old custom for the captain to do this when we have suffered a defeat.'

They seemed to like it.

We all had a few to drink that night and became a bit loud and rowdy. I was rooming with Denis and back upstairs, as we lurched around, I knocked a marble table over and it smashed. The hotel people were a little unhappy at this. Back home, the next day, the papers were full of reports about us and other players wrecking their hotel rooms. This sort of behaviour was unheard of then – it was ten years before The Who and other rock bands became famous for launching television sets off hotel balconies. But it did not happen at all. I expect a reporter phoned his news desk when he saw Denis and I getting a ticking off and made the familiar tabloid mountain out of a molehill.

The air of expectancy at Spurs had spread to the supporters. Over 50,000 turned up for our first League game against Everton in August 1960. We won 2–0. Bill Nicholson had lifted us before the game when he said in his usual calm and understated way, 'I was disappointed we did not win the Championship last year. We were good enough, but it was not to be. I think if we simply carry on where we left off, we will this season. Good luck, gentlemen, and enjoy yourselves.'

And did we enjoy ourselves. We won the next ten games, making a record-winning sequence of eleven matches, scoring thirty-six goals and only conceding eleven. It was fantastic. The twelfth match we drew and then we won another four on the spin. We were running away with it. We almost had the Championship in the bag by Christmas. Only Billy Wright's Wolves team and Sheffield Wednesday were close. At the halfway point, we had won eighteen matches, drawn two and lost one. An amazing 38 points out of a possible 42. With each game, our play got better and we looked unbeatable. We practically were. Only Sheffield Wednesday (again) managing to do it before Christmas. The football was beautiful and delighted purists of the game like Bill Nicholson, Danny Blanchflower and myself. We all believed strongly that if people spent their hard-earned money coming to watch a football match, they deserved to be – and should be – entertained. At Spurs, we certainly did that. I can never recall playing for a draw. I can never remember plotting to take someone out and we never turned nasty as a team when we were beaten. When another club played well against us, we appreciated it. We would often comment about the skills and abilities of opponents.

Bill was a lover of good football and so was Danny; they inspired and influenced the rest of us.

Being in a brilliant footballing side is a great thing. Most professional footballers are lucky enough to play in a good side at some point in their careers; few are fortunate enough to be part of a great, great side and, when you are, the satisfaction and pride is immense. Great sides do not last long, are hard to build – and even harder to maintain – but when they click, everyone knows it and whatever happens in the future, nobody can take it away from you. We felt like a conquering army smothering and bamboozling the enemy with skill and ingenuity, each player looking out for the other, supremely confident of one another's abilities. Bill Brown was on top form. Gordon Banks had not yet established himself so, at the time, Brown was certainly the best goalkeeper on these islands. The full-backs Peter Baker and Ron Henry were accomplished, calm and collected, raising their game to levels they probably never dreamt of. Big Maurice Norman at centre-half was having a whale of a time charging up for corners and generally causing mayhem whilst winning everything in the air in defence. Danny and I were roving wing-halves pushing up when we could, holding the line and feeding balls to John White, Les Allen and Bobby Smith up front. Cliff Jones, Terry Dyson and Terry Medwin raided from the flanks, also feeding the hungry head and feet of Bobby Smith. Bobby managed 28 goals in that historic season and Les Allen hit the net 23 times.

Bobby was on fire. My favourite ever goal is one I saw him score for England against Spain in October 1960. I was a spectator in the crowd. The Spanish goalkeeper had a habit of coming off his line and Bobby cheekily lobbed him, leaving the keeper helpless, running backward and squirming as the ball rolled into the net. For a man who was known as a big, bustling, no-nonsense centre-forward, it was exquisite. I have never seen the goal since (perhaps the BBC has binned the reel), but it was absolute class.

In the November during this breathtaking domestic run, Danny and I found ourselves on opposite sides in an international match between Scotland and Northern Ireland. It was a good Irish line-up, boasting Harry Gregg, survivor and hero of the Munich air disaster, in goal, Alex Elder in defence and Peter McParland up front. I was heartened that the Scottish side won with a convincing 5–2. I really felt that the national side was coming together well. Ralph Brand, our old pal from school, who I remember used to come to our house and play our old piano, played and scored that day, as did Denis Law and Alex Young. Making his debut in midfield was a boy from Rangers called Jim Baxter. He was excellent and I felt we could build a young side around him. I looked forward to the next England match with relish. Little did I know what was coming.

It was a good Christmas. We were settled now in London. The kids were young. We were affluent and bigger things were around the corner. Elvis Presley was top of the hit parade with 'It's Now or Never' and I knew it was now. Tottenham Hotspur would surrender their leadership of the First Division over my dead body. My profile had risen rapidly. It would be unusual to pick up a newspaper and not find something about me inside. The sports pages, I hasten to add. My reputation as a hard man in the game was growing, although this was something I did not nurture. I naturally preferred it when journalists focused on my ball control, my passing, my long throws or my goal scoring. But I did accept, and was proud, that my main attributes were my tackling, commitment and hopefully my leadership. Nevertheless, Dave Mackay rarely got mentioned without the words 'square-jawed', 'barrel-chested', 'hard-tackling', 'craggy' and 'fearsome' appearing in close proximity. Whatever the style, the crowds and the public seemed to like it and I found I was becoming instantly recognisable. People approached me in the street and asked me for my autograph and whether I was in Tottenham, the West End of London or wherever, they were always charming. Newspapers were tipping me for the Football Writers' Association Footballer of the Year award and I was astounded when, in December 1960, I was voted fifth in a sports personality of the year poll. John Surtees, the motor racing driver, won it and Stirling Moss was breathing down his neck. Gold medallist runner Brian Hewson was third and Bobby Charlton fourth.

The Spurs side in general were attracting a great deal of press attention at the time and the following article from a national newspaper, which I reproduce below, could well have been the first about the enviable lifestyles of footballers:

£5,000 HOUSE AND A JAG IN THE GARAGE

Davie Mackay rolls up in his Jaguar. Bill Brown steps out of a modern £5,000 house. John White enjoys regular theatre shows and slap-up dinners – free of charge.

It probably sounds like something out of the Arabian Nights. But it's the real thing all right. For this is the fabulous world into which these three Scots have stepped today – simply by belonging to Tottenham Hotspur – the 'Millionarios' of British football.

Tot-Hot are the Super-Leaguers. They've started the season with a record ten wins on the trot. They're heading for the League title and the talent money that goes with it. They're rated certs for next season's European Cup. And already players are cashing in on every opportunity.

In fact, if Messrs Mackay, White and Brown had rubbed Aladdin's lamp, they couldn't have come out much better. They and their mates are really reaping the benefit of those top-class displays on the field. While gates are falling almost everywhere in England, the Spurs are packing them in wherever they play – nearly half a million have watched their ten matches so far. And many happy customers are showing their appreciation in the most practical – and most acceptable – manner possible!

No Tottenham player needs to pay for a haircut. A local barber does the job free for the custom it brings to his shop. A butcher regularly supplies free meat. A fan owns a restaurant and supplies free meals. Another owns a ticket agency and slips them free seats for West End shows. Cliff Jones gets his car serviced free of charge. Danny Blanchflower has free tickets for the biggest fights in town.

And all the boys can get the odd shirt or two at trade prices.

Davie Mackay and Bill Brown are regularly in demand for signed newspaper articles and advertising endorsements. Cliff Jones advertises energy tablets and was recently taken to Spain so that he could study Real Madrid. Danny Blanchflower is probably the highest-paid footballer in the British game thanks to his on-the-side income. He's a newspaper columnist. He has his name on a football annual. He's a TV regular – as a personality and a commentator. He advertises a breakfast food and his own brand of football boots.

And, of course, like all the rest of the White Hart Lane, he gets everything that can be legally offered under the maximum wages scheme: £20 a week during the playing season, £17 in the summer, £4 win bonuses in League matches, TV match fees, £50 full-international fees, £20 inter-League matches fees. Most of the players live in modern £5,000 houses provided by the club. Most run cars – with Davie Mackay and his Jaguar taking pride of place.

No wonder they're calling 'em the 'Real Madrid of Britain'.

Re-reading this 40 years later, do I detect shades of prejudice against Scots, professional jealousy about Danny Blanchflower and the now familiar shock-horror reaction to the lot of professional footballers? What about Cliff Jones getting his car serviced free of charge? I didn't know about that – lucky he was not charged with bringing the game into disrepute.

In the New Year, we knocked Charlton Athletic out of the FA Cup in the third round and were drawn at home to Crewe Alexandra, yet again, in the fourth. It was a surprise to me that lining up for Crewe that night was my old best pal and colleague from the Saughton School football team Terry Tighe. We won 5–1 and both Terry and I got on the score sheet. Crewe played tenaciously that night, but if it hadn't been for a superhuman performance from their goalkeeper, it could have been another 13–2. Terry stayed around and came for a drink with me and some of the lads after the game. Over 50,000 had watched us play that cold, dark evening. We had come a long way from the playing fields of Saughton School. Much went unsaid that evening. In footballing terms, my best days were still to come and Terry had played his. Such is the roller-coaster life of a professional footballer, where luck can count for so much. As lads, there was nothing to choose between Terry Tighe and me. I have no doubt he could have been a top defender in the English First Division too. But the breaks didn't fall to him. He had just escaped from Accrington Stanley before joining Crewe. Stanley were a League club with a long history but had been forced to sell their best players to stave off bankruptcy. It was too late and in 1962 they disappeared altogether. (They have, however, re-emerged in recent years.) A stark reminder to us all of how precarious life could be at the bottom of the football pile.

We were the talk of the town. The Championship looked sewn up and, after defeating Crewe and moving into the fifth round of the FA Cup, people started to talk seriously about Spurs winning the Double. We had been drawn against Danny's old club Aston Villa and were fancied strongly to progress from there into the quarter-finals. At White Hart Lane, we parried such talk with the age-old line that we were taking one game at a time, but the truth was, from Crewe onwards, we wanted the Double more than anything.

In February, we were told that the BBC were planning to surprise our captain, Danny Blanchflower, and make him the subject of their highly popular *This Is Your Life* programme. On the day, us players were bussed to some BBC studios to await Danny, who was being collared by his fellow-countryman Eamonn Andrews elsewhere. He never showed. Danny was the first person to refuse the big red book and literally ran away. As far as he was concerned, this was *his* life and he was keeping it that way. We had a party anyway with his family, old friends and assorted other footballers. I felt a bit of an idiot because I had told some friends and family of my own to tune in to the TV for a surprise that evening. I told them as I tapped the side of my nose that I was not in a position to reveal any more. Their confusion was only increased when they sat through an episode of *This Is Your Life* featuring a dear old man who had fostered scores of children!

Much was made of Danny's reaction and many media commentators applauded what they saw as his stand against the creeping intrusion of television into people's private lives. Personally, I felt that Danny would have enjoyed such a tribute and that his reasons for refusing had more to do with his private life than his principles. He and Betty were having marital problems at the time and my guess is Danny could not entertain the hypocrisy that the programme might entail.

He did, however, go on John Freeman's extraordinary *Face to Face* programme. The modern-day chat show bears little relation to this programme where celebrities subjected themselves to direct and raw questioning from Freeman. It was compulsive viewing, with a close-up camera on the guest's face throughout. Danny came out well, as did Adam Faith, a young pop star of the time who sticks in my mind from another edition. The programme, though, is best remembered now for Gilbert Harding's emotional breakdown when quizzed about his late parents. This was all the more remarkable as Gilbert had achieved TV stardom through playing up his unsympathetic, crotchety character on shows such as *What's My Line?*

Back on the pitch, we experienced the inevitable wobble. We lost the first game of 1961 to Manchester United at Old Trafford and then succumbed to Leicester City at home two weeks later. In March, there were defeats to Cardiff City and Newcastle United. Suddenly, the gap between us in first position and Sheffield Wednesday in second was only three points. We did have the excuse of the FA Cup, though, where we were progressing nicely. Aston Villa were overcome and then we were up against Second Division Sunderland in the quarter-finals. Obviously we were favourites, even if the tie was at Roker Park.

People can get very romantic about football crowds and many have spoken and written about the famous Roker Roar, but it was true – the noise that home crowd made was unique. It was not at all hostile, but it was a roar of huge rumbling volume that unsettled visitors and lifted the home side immeasurably. It was practically tangible. I have not visited Sunderland's new ground, the Stadium of Light, but I hope for their sakes that somehow they managed to take the Roker Roar with them when they moved location. With help from the roar and a sterling performance from their young team, we were held to a 1–1 draw in front of 60,000 that March day in 1961.

Without their passionate home support, when Sunderland came down for the replay, the gap between the Divisions showed and they were systematically crushed. I scored the last goal in a 5–0 win. We knew by then we were facing Burnley in ten days' time in the semi-final to be held at Villa Park.

Burnley were the side we didn't want to meet until Wembley. We had a healthy respect for them. They were the League champions and, like Sheffield Wednesday, were tough and better than most at containing us. Earlier in the season, they had staged a remarkable comeback at White Hart Lane when they fought like tigers from 4–0 down to draw 4–4. That had showed their mettle. With players like John Angus, an England international, Alex Elder, Jimmy Adamson and Danny's friend and fellow Irish hero, Jimmy McIlroy, they had their biggest assets in defence and the middle of the field. Up front, though, were England stars winger John Connelly and target man Ray Pointer, both top players and very capable of causing problems for anyone.

Now we were all talking about the Double openly and generally agreed that this tie was the crucial one. The other semi-finalists – Sheffield United and Leicester City – held little fear for us. We were as nervous about Burnley as they were, I'm sure, about us. We could smell the Double even though our form in the second half of the season had become less emphatic and we felt beating Burnley would take us within a whisker. If we could do that, we just had to keep our heads. Danny addressed us as captain before the game: 'We should win this. We are the better side. Just. But we need to keep calm and collected. Get through this and we will take the Double. I'm sure of it.'

A few days before the tie, Burnley were themselves knocked out of the European Cup by Hamburg and this pleased us. We hoped their spirit might be broken, but we soon found out that this was not the case. It was not a great flowing game, as both teams played cautiously, afraid of making mistakes and burdened by the implications of defeat. If anything, Burnley shaded us in the first half and we were fortunate to score when Bobby Smith poked a Les Allen pass into Adam Blacklaw's net. We were even luckier when Burnley had a goal disallowed almost straight from the second-half whistle. Had it stood, I think we would have been looking at a replay at least. But that sapped them a little and we were able to capitalise with another from Bobby and, towards the end of the game, a third goal scored by Cliff Jones. It was a very flattering scoreline. The Tottenham hordes that had made the journey up from London invaded the pitch and mobbed Bobby in particular. He deserved it. It had taken 40 years, but Spurs were now in the FA Cup final, their first at Wembley. Leicester City, whom we had beaten home and away already during the season, were to be our opponents.

Back in the League, we had the business of securing the Championship before concentrating on winning the FA Cup final and therefore the Double. We didn't start too well. Somehow we lost to Newcastle, who were struggling at the foot of the division. Their goalkeeper, Dave Hollins, whose younger brother John would later make his name at Chelsea, played probably the finest game of his career in keeping us at bay. He'd have caught Ronald Biggs that day. Then we faced Fulham at Craven Cottage and my nemesis Johnny Haynes controlled proceedings. We were lucky to leave there with a draw. Sheffield Wednesday were still knocking on the Championship door. Our ten-point lead at Christmas had been whittled down, so we were just a few ahead. We began to fret. Bill Nicholson did as well and gave us a talking to. He was calm and polite, as always, but he made the point that our forwards were not capitalising on their chances as they should have been and as they had done previously. I didn't agree. Our defence had also been slipping. We were letting in more goals. But the talk helped or our luck changed – we went out and won the next four matches, notching up fifteen more goals. On 17 April 1961, we faced Sheffield

Wednesday at home and now all we needed was a draw to become League champions. Wednesday needed to win to stay in with a chance of catching us.

It was another gutsy, bone-crunching game and one where we did not (could not) play the sort of football that had got us to the point we were at. I was booked and had chunks kicked out of my legs. Cliff Jones required stitches. Even Bobby Smith was battered and bruised. But we were giving it out in spades too, such was the determination from both sides to prevail. A 62,000-strong crowd packed into the ground that evening, forsaking Ena Sharples and *Coronation Street* and probably blissfully unaware that on the other side of the world President John Kennedy was dicing with world peace by launching the Bay of Pigs invasion on Fidel Castro's Cuba. Anyway, there were far more important things to worry about than the survival of the planet.

Wednesday's England international forward John Fantham managed to break the deadlock in the first half and when that was followed shortly after by their centre-forward hitting the post, we were rocked. But we kept our heads. Danny Blanchflower was superb, a sleek Afghan hound among a field full of barking terriers, slowing the game down and forcing us to take control. Just before the half-time whistle, we scored twice. Bobby Smith and Les Allen again.

We came out for the second half resolute. We would not surrender this hard-fought lead and, although the last 10 minutes seemed to tick by slower than the first 35, we managed to hang on. When the whistle blew, I remember just stopping on the spot and drinking in the jubilation of the crowd before dashing for the changing-rooms as people tumbled onto the pitch like a dam bursting. Somehow, with our white shirts highly conspicuous among the dark clothing of the hordes, we all made it inside, grinning and panting as we sought cover. Bill Nick, Cecil Poynton and Harold Evans were already in there shaking our hands and patting our backs as we passed through. We hugged each other and jumped up and down. Outside on the pitch, the crowd had congregated underneath the directors' box.

'We want Danny. We want Danny,' they chanted. Louder and

louder as more joined the throng.

Danny seemed faintly embarrassed. I was facing him, smiling broadly.

Someone from behind placed his hand on our captain's shoulder and squeezed it. 'Come on, Danny boy, the pipes are calling.' And he looked at me as great gobs of tears came from nowhere and clouded his eyes.

Champions with three games remaining, the rest of the League programme was an anti-climax. Bill Nicholson wanted us to win those and take the Championship with the highest amount of points ever. So did we, but none of us players were going to risk injury and the prospect of not playing in the Cup final. We lost two of the three remaining matches, but still managed to finish eight points clear of runners-up Sheffield Wednesday. No team had taken the title by a bigger margin since Manchester United won it by nine points in 1908. We won a record thirty-one games out of forty-two during the campaign and our eleven-match winning sequence was also a record in the First Division. Danny Blanchflower had been voted Footballer of the Year for the second time and now we had the Cup final ahead of us to set up even more records.

Before that, I had a rather important international match to deal with. As I said earlier, I felt that Scotland were coming together nicely and, buoyed by our League Championship and Double prospects, I really felt that we could beat England on 15 April at Wembley stadium. Remember, I was getting quite accustomed to things going right for me. A young player by the name of Greaves was in the England side and he linked up front with our very own Bobby Smith, who like me was a newly crowned champion, full of swagger and confidence. England were dynamite from the kick-off and stunned us with their attacking play. I know I would say this, but the side they fielded that day was the best England team I have ever seen, including the one that would go on to win the World Cup five years later. Ron Springett from our old enemy Sheffield Wednesday kept the goal, Jimmy Armfield and Mick McNeil were the full-backs and Peter Swan, Ron Flowers and

Bobby Robson held the halfway line. The forward line consisted of Bryan Douglas, Johnny Haynes, Bobby Charlton, Bobby Smith and young Mr Greaves. Bobby Robson scored inside ten minutes and Jimmy Greaves, the most natural goalscorer I had ever seen (and would ever see) got another two to put the home side 3–0 up at half-time.

In the dressing-room during the break, recriminations flew. We were devastated to find ourselves in this position at half-time. I remember thinking that if we did not pull ourselves together, we were in danger of being really massacred – the thought was one I could not entertain. I ran back out on that hallowed Wembley turf like a man possessed. We were determined to pull the game back by sheer force of will if nothing else. I scored within three minutes and Davie Wilson followed five minutes later. Suddenly it was 3–2 and we were back in it. The relief was palpable. Then England got a free kick and Bryan Douglas took it quickly. Too quickly for our goalkeeper Frank Haffey, who caught the ball but dropped it like a piece of burnt toast and watched it bobble into the net. That was it. We buckled and England scored a stratospheric five goals in twelve minutes. Somewhere amongst the mayhem, we managed to score once more. It was inconsequential. We were routed like we had never been routed before and like we never will be again. It was like we were a Sunday park side who happened by some quirk of fate to be playing Brazil at their peak. We were spectators of our own destruction. Jimmy Greaves got another couple to make a hat-trick. Bobby Smith got two, as did Johnny Haynes. I prayed for the final whistle.

In footballing terms, it was the worst day of my life. Afterwards, in the dressing-room, there was no inquest. There was simply nothing to say at that point. We were all in shock. Almost as if we had been hit by a car. History has blamed our goalkeeper, Frank Haffey, but this is far too simplistic. For a goalkeeper to concede nine goals, his defence must have failed at least nine times, too. That was us. We played crap. Frank played double crap. I felt such shame for letting my country down so dramatically and did not know how I could face anyone. After the game, Denis Law and I decided we needed to take solace in alcohol and sneaked into the West End for drinks at Malcolm Allison's 142 Club. Alcohol began to deaden the senses until we turned and looked over our shoulders to see half of the England team, all smiles and bathed in the glow of victory, walking in the door.

For opposite reasons, the game ranks as one of the most famous in English and Scottish soccer history. After-dinner tales have sprung up around Frank Haffey in particular. The press dubbed him 'Slap-Haffey' and 'Nine past Haffey' and claimed he joked afterwards about 'liking one over the eight'. If he said that, it was not in front of me. Denis Law tells of how he met him in Australia decades later (sensibly, Frank emigrated soon after the match) and Frank asked meekly, 'Denis, is it safe to come home yet?' For myself, I am regularly asked about the game, wherever in the world I might be.

'You played in the 9–3 game, didn't you?'

'No.'

'Oh, I thought you did. I could have sworn I remember you playing.'

'I was on the pitch, granted, but I didn't play.'

Thank God for the FA Cup and the prospect of the Double to allow me the opportunity, like governments since, to bury bad news. We booked in at the Hendon Hall Hotel on the Friday afternoon before the game and then travelled to Wembley Stadium so Bill could acquaint us with the playing surface. I was only too well acquainted, thank you, Bill. In the evening, we boarded a coach for the West End of London, where Bill had arranged for us to see the film *The Guns of Navarone*. I don't remember much about it except it was a war film and David Niven, Stanley Baker and Gregory Peck were in it. I'm not sure if I cannot recall anything else because the film wasn't very good or because my mind was elsewhere.

We were happily tired by the time we got back to Hendon Hall and went off to bed and sleep. I was rooming with Bill Brown and we both got up that morning at our leisure. Downstairs, most of the lads were in the television room perched on chairs watching

Grandstand and the build-up to the final. Even if you weren't personally involved, it was impossible not to get caught up in the general enthusiasm of commentators David Coleman, Kenneth Wolstenholme and Raymond Glendenning. The FA Cup final in England really does cross over into mainstream life more than any other sporting occasion. The shops, roads and streets empty on this Saturday afternoon in May. I am told that, bar Christmas, it is the only afternoon in the year that a car can lap the M25 and average over 50 mph. That is now. It was bigger then. For us, the excitement just built and built, especially as our team coach neared the twin towers of Wembley and thousands of supporters from both clubs jammed the road, most bedecked with rosettes and wearing team-coloured hats and carrying rattles, trumpets and the like.

All players lucky enough to have played in an FA Cup final will tell you that there is nothing like that moment when you leave the tunnel and emerge out onto the sun-kissed lush turf. The noise is deafening and the singing, swaying, brightly coloured crowd a sight to behold. You really don't want it to end. I ran up and down and jumped on the spot like a boxer waiting for the fight to start. I clapped my hands together and shouted encouragement to the other lads. In 90 minutes, we could have made history. It's hard to stay calm when you're looking it in the face.

Tottenham had been made strong favourites to win the game, but Leicester were no pushovers. They had beaten us 3–2 at White Hart Lane, although we had beaten them 2–1 at Filbert Street. The season before, they had taken the points again at home and we drew up there. This season they had also inflicted a 6–0 thrashing on Manchester United. They had some good players, including young Gordon Banks in goal, Frank McLintock in defence and Ken Leek up front. We were heartened when we discovered that Leek was not playing. Bizarrely, he had been dropped.

As the game started, the sun from earlier in the day hid behind clouds and rain started to fall. It seemed to cast a pall over the match and both sides got a bit bogged down in scrappy and disjointed football. It was about even in terms of possession and chances when Les Allen caught Leicester's Len Chalmers with a

1. The Mackay Brothers. Standing, from left to right, myself and Tommy; sitting, from left to right, Ronnie and Frank.

2. My parents, Thomas and Catherine Mackay, pictured outside our home in Glendevon Park, Edinburgh, where I grew up.

3. The triumphant Saughton School team. That's me standing on the far right.

4. Hearts players before the historic 1956 Scottish Cup final victory. From left to right: Ian Crawford, unknown, Freddie Glidden, myself, Tam McKenzie, John Cumming, Willie Bauld, Johnny Harvey, Jimmy Wardhaugh and Alex Young.

5. Happy as a lark having joined my beloved Hearts.

6. Danny Blanchflower before Spurs' 1962 FA Cup final. Jimmy Greaves, John White and I appreciate Prince Philip's joke. Peter Purves, in the background, does not.

7. Training with Scotland: manager Matt Busby explains a point.

8. Andy Beattie, Scotland manager, ticks Bill Brown, Denis Law and me off for being late for a game against Wales.

9. Can you spot me? Bet you can't. This is the FA Cup final penalty where Danny Blanchflower wanted me to join him in a 'spectacular', but I chickened out and ran away. (© Reuters)

| 10 |
| 11 | 12 |

10. The Tottenham Hotspur Double side in training. Someone has told us that the Arsenal team bus is just passing outside! (© Photonews)

11. Practising my ball control.

12. Happy days with John and Sandra White. Isobel is trying to persuade me to drink more vinegar.

13. Collecting my third FA Cup with Spurs in 1967. This one was the sweetest as I was captain and had just recovered from my two broken legs.

14. Sidelined and plastered. My boys and I watching Spurs with my first broken leg. (© *Sport and General*)

15. Slimline tonic. Brian Clough (left) took me to Derby and gave my playing career the lease of life I never thought possible. (© *Daily Mirror*)

16. Derby v. Spurs: Mackay v. Mullery. Old Spurs captain meets new Spurs captain. (© *Derby Evening Telegraph*)

17. Relaxing with Marty Feldman. From left: myself, Bobby Smith, Marty and Jimmy Greaves. (© Hy Money)

18. The family in the 1970s. Left to right: Derek, nephew Douglas, myself, Dad, Isobel, Valerie, David and Julie.

19. Celebrating winning the League as manager with Derby. Left to right: Des Anderson, Archie Gemmill and myself.

20. With Dad and Joe Kinnear in Dubai.

21. Trophies in Egypt.

22. Spot the legend. There are not many missing at this historic football dinner.

23. Survivors of the Double side and Bill Nicholson. There is a campaign to have Bill Nick knighted. Nobody in football is more deserving of this honour.

tackle that really hurt him. It was an accident, but may have looked like it wasn't. Len was hurt really badly and, had there been substitutes at the time, he would certainly have been taken off. Instead he remained on the pitch, an invalid limping around. With Leicester effectively down to ten men we should have taken them apart, but we did not. City raised their game and matched us man for man, which was quite something when there were ten of them and eleven of us. Shortly before half-time, Cliff Jones managed to put one past Gordon Banks but the goal was ruled offside.

I cannot remember what Bill Nicholson said to us during the break. Whatever it was, it would have been very little. He was not in the habit of shouting, bawling and swearing. He would have been calm and encouraging. He would have drawn our attention to some specifics. He would have seen things we hadn't. He would not have wanted us to change what we were doing, just to do it better. Personally, I decided that I would be taking no chances in moving forward and that I would stay deep in our half and focus purely on defending. We had a one-man advantage. We had five brilliant forwards. They didn't need me or Danny today. We'd help ensure that the door remained firmly closed. Bobby, Cliff, Les, Terry and John would have to do their stuff.

In the 70th minute they did. We finally broke the deadlock when wee Terry Dyson found an unmarked Bobby Smith with a glorious pass and good old Bobby turned and smashed it into the net. At last, we clicked into gear and took full advantage of Leicester's misery and understandable fatigue. We started to pass the ball as sharply and accurately as we could and began to surge forward. Ten minutes later, Bobby Smith was able to return the compliment when he sent in a cross that Terry Dyson met with his head and thumped solidly past the diving Banks. We knew then we'd done it. We only had to survive ten minutes and the chances of Leicester getting two in that time were negligible. We knew it. Leicester knew it. The crowd knew it and the millions watching at home knew it. The final whistle, when it came, was a formality.

Like when we won the League, the immediate celebrations have become a bit of a blur in my memory. I recall climbing the legendary 39 steps to collect my medal and Danny holding the Cup aloft. I remember running around the pitch to salute the fans and posing for the photographs I have seen so many times since. But I cannot remember what we said to one another. I do remember back in the changing-rooms with the champagne flowing and Bill Nicholson came among us and said something along the lines of it being a great achievement, but he was disappointed we didn't play the lovely football he knew we could. That took the wind out of my sails. Here was a man whose rise in football was nothing short of meteoric. A man who, in just 30 months, had fashioned a struggling First Division side into a team to take the first Double since before Queen Victoria died and he was expressing disappointment. He had created the so-called 'Team of the Century' yet he was nagged by the fact that, on the day we finally scaled the mountain, we did not play at the pinnacle of our abilities and thrill the watching millions. That's a perfectionist for you.

We had a dinner dance that evening at The Savoy in London and we drank champagne and danced the night away with our wives and girlfriends. Les Allen was not enjoying himself as fully as he should have been because he felt bad about the injury he had caused to Len Chalmers. Apparently, he had tried to offer apologies and condolences in the Leicester dressing-room after the game and had received short shrift. It probably wasn't the right time. After the meal, a number of telegrams were read out and one was from Len Chalmers saying 'Forget about it – Congratulations!' Les visibly relaxed after that fine example of sportsmanship from Len warmed all of us.

After the meal, I sat down next to John White. He had had a good game and a great season. His whole life had changed dramatically. Far more than mine.

'Glad you came down to London, John?'

'Oh, yes, Dave.' His eyes were dancing. I had never seen a happier man.

CHAPTER NINE

Kings of Europe

We were different after the Double. It gave us a new identity. I was no longer Dave Mackay, transfer from Hearts – I was Dave Mackay, part of the Double-winning side. We all were. The fuss was enormous. Spurs were the centre of the footballing universe and we were hailed as the Team of the Century, future conquerors of Europe and the saviours of British football. Advertising, sponsorship and book deals were offered. Stanley Paul, the publishers, approached me and, working with journalist Bryon Butler, we rushed out my book *Soccer My Spur*. A mad Spurs fan called Jimmy Burton asked me about putting my name to a rag-trade business he had. He called it Dave Mackay Ties and it survives to this day. I regret that I agreed to a lifetime's supply of neckwear for me and my family rather than negotiate a financial interest. Still, in a good year, I do get silk ones.

At home, Isobel was becoming frustrated with our house in Southgate. Nice as it was, with five of us living there, it was too small. Isobel was bending my ear daily. One morning, as I set off for training, I said dismissively, 'Look, if you don't like it, ring

Bill Nick.' I didn't dream she'd do just that and was mightily embarrassed when I found out she had. The club were great and Alan Leather, the secretary, bent over backwards to help us find a place. A friend steered us in the direction of 6 The Glade in Enfield. It was a lovely house with a big kitchen and a split-level lounge that seemed to us like a dance floor. The problem was that Tottenham would subsidise homes up to a price ceiling of £4,250 and this house was £7,250. Isobel was smitten and promised me we would never have another cross word if we could get it. Fortunately, the club readily agreed to help us finance the property, even though we were told to say, if asked, that we had financed the £3,000 excess ourselves.

I became great friends with Terry Dyson, Micky Dulin and Bobby Smith particularly and, after the match on a Saturday, we'd often go for drinks in the Bell and Hare, go dog racing at Walthamstow and then on to the West End to a club. One afternoon, Terry came round to the house in Southgate to show off his new Ford Zephyr and take me off to a boxing match. I was upstairs in the bedroom getting ready to join Terry for a spin when I noticed from the window the car beginning to roll across the road. To my horror, I realised our little boys had climbed in and must have released the handbrake. I leapt down the stairs and onto the road, but thankfully the car had come to a halt after bumping into a neighbour's parked car. I inspected the kids, Terry inspected his car and Isobel placated the neighbour.

We awaited the new season with keen excitement. We believed that the best was yet to come and that we could be the first British club to win the European Cup. That was our main aim. We'd won everything we could domestically so it was natural that we wanted to make more history and prove we were the best not just in Britain but in Europe as well. We felt that our style of play had more in common with European sides than most English clubs. Bill had given us a tremendous vote of confidence by not signing any new players in the close season. Danny, at 35 years of age, must have wondered if anyone was going to be brought in to fill his boots. Our first match of the season would have given him further hope because up at Bloomfield Road playing for

Blackpool in our 2–1 victory was Stanley Matthews, who was still jinking his way down the flanks at age 45. He was the exception rather than the rule – only a handful of on-field players have ever managed to play in First Division football beyond 40 but Danny, with his unbridled optimism and confidence, would have felt that as a defender he could last longer than Stan and probably envisaged bowing out gracefully sometime in the 1970s.

In September, we travelled to Poland for our first ever European Cup tie. Gornik Zabrze were not a famous side and Poland not then a significant footballing nation. I think we believed passing through the round would be a formality, but were rudely awakened by the passion of their near 100,000 crowd and the raw determination of the Poles to beat us. At half-time, we were trailing 3–0 and, as we shaped ourselves at the beginning of the second half, we conceded again. Our European hopes looked to be stymied at the first hurdle. Even if we held the line now, winning by five clear goals in the second leg would be a tall order. Their left-half was injured in a tackle with me and was forced to leave the pitch. This was a turning point for us and we managed to pull two goals back. Better, but we still had it all to do at White Hart Lane.

The replay a week later ranks as one of the best games I have ever played in. Zabrze were not a poor side and the scoreline of 8–1 encourages observers to dismiss them as early European Cup cannon fodder. We were irresistible on the night. We played the sort of game that Bill would have liked us to have played against Leicester City in the Cup final. It was an exhibition of the Double side at its best. Cliff Jones was superb and scored a hat-trick. Danny himself got on the score sheet as did Bobby Smith (twice), Terry Dyson and John White.

In the next round, we were drawn against Dutch side Feyenoord, whom we had beaten in a pre-season friendly. We managed to defeat them in Holland and drew at home to move into the next round, where we were drawn to play Dukla Prague, a side we knew little about, but were expected to give us less trouble than Gornik Zabrze or Feyenoord. The semi-finals beckoned and, after an early wobble, our European Cup prospects were looking good. Indeed, we didn't dare speak its name yet, but the Treble was beginning to look like a serious possibility. Our League form had not been as explosive as the previous season, but we were up there and no other club was running away with it as we had done, and the FA Cup campaign was yet to start.

I became more convinced we could do it when Bill Nicholson swooped in and signed Jimmy Greaves shortly before Christmas 1961. I had played against Jimmy when he was at Chelsea and when he had played for England, and he had never had a bad game. Like Denis Law, he tried his luck in Italy, but had been unhappy. Bill had paid AC Milan £99,999 for him. Bill was a pound shy to prevent Jimmy from carrying the burden of being the first £100,000 player. At that time, Jimmy was the best player in the country and if Bill had said to me that he had £100,000 to spend and asked who he should buy, I would have said Jimmy. No doubt. He made his debut against Blackpool and promptly scored a hat-trick, immediately starting a love affair with the Tottenham fans that survives to this day. During that second half of the season, he was like a man possessed, scoring an incredible 30 goals for us.

After Christmas, the fixtures started to pile up as we pressed ahead in the three competitions. We put Birmingham City and Plymouth Argyle out of the FA Cup. Then we travelled to Czechoslovakia and lost 1–0 to Dukla Prague in the first leg. On the following Saturday, we beat West Bromwich Albion in the fifth round of the Cup to move into the quarter-finals and then it was Prague again in the second leg.

It was played on a bitterly cold February night and the pitch was covered with a sheet of ice on which rested a carpet of fluffy snow. It seemed impossible that the game could be played in those conditions, but it was. A great one. Prague were good and played deft, passing football, as they had showed us in the first leg. Tony Marchi had deputised for me when I had been injured and he kept his place. Bill played me at inside-left and I revelled in it. Within minutes of starting, I had a goal disallowed. Bobby Smith compensated an instant later with a real one and from then on we dominated the game. I scored two goals in my forward position in the 4–1 victory, but everyone had a good game. John White and Cliff Jones, I remember vividly, looked like they had been designed to play on ice. Watching them reminded me of ice-skaters, not footballers. Full of grace, poise and beauty.

The momentum built. We beat Aston Villa in the FA Cup quarter-finals to reach the semi-final point and our opponents would be Manchester United at Hillsborough. In the European Cup, we were up against Benfica of Portugal, with their world superstar Eusebio, in the semis. Their coach declared that whoever won the tie would win the European Cup. He was right. Thus, in March 1962, with hindsight, our team was probably at its absolute peak. Still well placed to retain the League title – a strong run-in would clinch it – and in the semi-finals of the European Cup and the FA Cup. So very, very near.

The first leg against Benfica was a very physical one and we were extremely unlucky to lose by 3–1. We had two perfectly good goals disallowed. One from Bobby Smith was ruled offside when the ball actually passed two defenders on its way to goal. Shortly before the end of the match, I hit the bar. We were all very disappointed to lose the game. We played as well as, if not better than, Benfica and still felt we could turn it around at home and reach the final.

Before that, we played our FA Cup semi-final against Manchester United. Matt Busby had done wonders with his decimated squad and United were a force again in English football – and they were going to get better and better. But at this point, they were no match for us and we won the tie comfortably. Jimmy Greaves set the tone in the opening minutes when he got on to a John White pass and slid the ball past the United goalkeeper. Further goals from Terry Medwin and Cliff Jones prevented United from getting back into it. In the other semi-final, Burnley had beaten Fulham. We'd have rather faced Fulham – Johnny Haynes or no Johnny Haynes – for Burnley were a side, like Sheffield Wednesday, with whom we had experienced problems. They too were in the League race and were snapping at leaders Ipswich's heels and us at theirs. Ipswich Town's rise had been unexpected and remarkable. Bill Nicholson's push-and-run colleague, Alf Ramsey, had taken over the little East Anglian club as manager and had propelled them upwards in a couple of seasons from the depths of the Second Division. With no spending power to speak of, this was amazing and throughout the season observers expected this anomalous situation to correct itself, but it didn't.

Nearly 65,000 jammed into White Hart Lane for the replay against Benfica and the fans were in full song, with the now trademark 'Glory, Glory, Tottenham Hotspur' anthem, sung to the tune of 'John Brown's Body', floating across north London. I was not in the team because of an injury, but the lads played a blinder without me. Jimmy Greaves had another perfectly good goal disallowed. Danny Blanchflower scored from a penalty and Bobby Smith bagged our second in the 2–1 victory. But it was not enough. Had Jimmy's goal stood, I'm sure we'd have prevailed. The match was shown live on television and the British public agreed it was amongst the finest they had ever witnessed; for us, it was bitterly disappointing. We'd fallen at the penultimate hurdle and hadn't deserved to. I was flattered, though, when I read in the papers afterwards that Eusebio had said I was the best all-round player in the world.

During our European and FA Cup campaigns, it was inevitable that we took our eye off the League ball. We had slipped back a little and during April we lost two crucial matches. One was against Ipswich Town at home. Now not only had we been pipped in Europe, but retaining the Championship looked impossible. However, with these distractions out of the way, we made a real end-of-season push and won three of our remaining games. It was not quite enough. Ipswich Town were the new League champions, Burnley were runners-up only three points behind and we were third, one point behind them. It was unthinkable that the best side in the land would finish the season empty-handed, so we knew we had to win the FA Cup again – not only to maintain some momentum and retain our pride, but also to ensure we would compete in Europe the following season.

We were not a team to mope and, although there was great regret that we had not been able to achieve the Treble or European glory, we soon put it behind us. We had been unlucky and we did not allow these setbacks to dent our self-confidence and belief in our abilities. Danny and I spent hours in training together discussing tactics, practising moves and improving ball control. One of the things we worked on was a little trick we had up our sleeve. Danny was our penalty-taker and we devised a move whereby, instead of striking his penalty kick at the goalkeeper, he would feign a shot but instead just tap the ball forward a foot or two. Once the goalkeeper had dived, I would step forward and place the ball on the other side of the goal mouth from where he had landed. It was pure theatre and showing off, but we wanted to do it and decided to unveil the move on the biggest stage.

'Are you up for it, Dave? If we get a penalty at Wembley against Burnley, we're going to go for it, yes?'

I nodded.

Danny was mad like that. Bill Nicholson would not have approved and if we mucked it up – God forbid. But Danny wanted to be part of one of the most famous goals in history. There was no satisfying the man.

The 1962 FA Cup final was the performance that Bill wanted the Leicester final the previous year to have been. Our pre-match drill was pretty much the same as the year before and only Jimmy Greaves among us hadn't been around last time. We felt like old hands and were not even slightly intimidated by the occasion. Because the television age was now well and truly upon us, with each year the FA Cup final was becoming a bigger and bigger event, transfixing the nation. Football was on the up. The England team were on their way to Chile to compete in the World Cup finals and would only succumb to Brazil and Pelé at the quarter-final stage. The M1 was by now open and fans were able to travel to away games in large numbers – and because disposable income was higher than ever for the working man, people were beginning to do just that. Soon *Match of the Day* would debut on BBC2 and supporters would be able to watch themselves, as well as their heroes, on prime-time television.

If we had been listening to our radios that morning in the hotel, Jimmy Young might have been playing 'Stranger on the Shore' by

Acker Bilk or 'Wonderful Land' by The Shadows, both instrumental numbers. The age of the beat group and The Beatles and The Rolling Stones was still a year away. If we had watched TV the night before with our families, we'd have been glued to *Z Cars*, the serial about policemen in fictional Newtown. It was the first police programme to portray working-class Britain in a slightly more realistic and gritty light than that which we had been used to. Little did we know that it would lead to *The Bill*, which would have us believe we are under siege in a land full of wife-beaters, drug addicts, paedophiles, murderers, perverts and arsonists. And that's just the police officers.

The game couldn't have started better. Jimmy Greaves, forever the poacher, prodded the ball past Adam Blacklaw in the Burnley goal after just 180 seconds. A goal at that stage in a Cup final is a godsend. The other team has it all to do psychologically and practically they need to push forward more than they would have, thus potentially leaving themselves vulnerable.

Burnley did pull level, though, soon after half-time with a goal from Jimmy Robson. We replied almost instantly when John White sent over a cross for Bobby Smith to hammer home. The game continued with us firmly on top, but with Burnley always dangerous. In the last ten minutes, a Burnley defender handled the ball in a goalmouth scramble and the referee blew for a penalty. Danny Blanchflower picked up the ball and looked around for me. He had that manic grin on his face. My stomach flipped as I realised this was the moment. We were a goal up with only six or seven minutes to play and would probably still win even if this impudent stunt of ours did not work. But what if we fluffed it? What if Burnley equalised and forced extra time? And won. The whole game turning on a penalty missed through two big-heads wanting to show off. Imagine if our piece of theatre led to Spurs not qualifying for Europe. The hand of history did not rest on my shoulder – it throttled me. I simply lost my bottle as they say. As I ran backwards to my half in retreat I gave a little shake of the head and kept running lest Danny chased me and dragged me back to the penalty spot. Danny didn't mind. It meant he had the honour of scoring a goal in an FA Cup final and he shimmied, sent

Blacklaw the wrong way and placed the ball in the back of the net. It was 3–1. We won the Cup.

The FA Charity Shield match played at the start of the season between the League winners and the FA Cup winners is not normally an ultra-competitive affair and is really a showcase and curtain-raiser to the new season (although Billy Bremner and Kevin Keegan thought differently when they brawled and were sent off some years later in a match between Leeds and Liverpool). However, against Ipswich Town at Portman Road on 11 August 1962, we felt we had something to prove. We believed that, had we not been distracted by Europe and the Cup, we would have retained the title and that we were certainly a better side than Alf Ramsey's Ipswich Town. We whipped them 5–1 and went into the 1962–63 season on a high note. Europe beckoned again, although this time we were in the not-quite-so-prestigious European Cup-Winners' Cup. Still, no British club had won it yet and it was the next best thing. We resolved to be the new Cup holders.

Spurs got off to a storming start in the League, winning five of the first six games. In the Cup-Winners' Cup, we were drawn against Glasgow Rangers in a match that many had hoped might have been the final. I was pleased and proud to be playing at Ibrox Park in my home country for the first time in a while and with this still fantastic and largely unaltered Spurs team. We had won the first leg at White Hart Lane 5–2 and were comfortable we would not relinquish our three-goal advantage, but that is not to say that the fanatical Glaswegian crowd did not try to intimidate us into surrendering. Early on, Jimmy Greaves took a pass from me and scored. There was no coming back from that. The aggregate score over the two legs ended up at 8–4. John White scored twice with his head, I recall, and Danny Blanchflower was injured. It emerged that he would need to have a cartilage removed. At the age of 37, there were doubts as to whether he would be able to come back before the end of the season, but he was back within a couple of months and was around for the all-important run-in.

The winter of 1962 was memorable for its deep, continuous snow, freezing cold and treacherous icy conditions. I believe it was far worse than anything we have seen in England since, yet I cannot recall any talk of climate change, approaching ice ages or the end of the world as tends to happen nowadays once the first slither of ice sticks to the first windscreen. It played havoc with the fixture list, but there were some memorable games on the domestic front. We trounced Nottingham Forest 9–2 and it could easily have been 18! Forest had been a goal up as well. Mr Greaves got four. The previous week, one of the Sunday writers had reacted to our defeat at Sheffield United by saying we were an ageing side and past our best. That had rankled and we keenly looked for his match report the following day.

In December, we played in a ding-dong match with Ron Greenwood's up-and-coming young West Ham side. It was an incredible 4–4 draw. A youthful Bobby Moore played with a maturity beyond his years. The match is memorable to me because I got the second hat-trick of my career and my only one at Spurs. Mind you, I was a defender. In January 1963, Burnley took revenge for the previous year's FA Cup final defeat and knocked us out in the third round. Yet, in the League, we were unbeaten between December and March and during that period put together a six-game winning streak. Along with Everton and Burnley, again, we led the pack.

We were a family club, as I have said before, and when around this time our assistant manager, Harry Evans, died, we were all devastated. He had complained of stomach pains and was admitted to hospital for investigative surgery. They found extensive cancer and, within a few weeks, Harry died. He was a lovely man and by then John White's father-in-law. It was all so sad. He and Bill had made a great managerial team.

The second-round Cup-Winners' Cup tie was less daunting than Rangers and we squarely beat Slovan Bratislava 6–2 on aggregate. Suddenly, we were in the semi-finals and OFK Belgrade of Yugoslavia were our opponents. I don't believe the team exists anymore. Come to that, neither does the country. They were very real on the night of our tie and, although we could play a physical game with the best of them, this little lot made it clear from the off that they preferred to kick us rather than the ball.

Jimmy Greaves created a new record that night: he became the first Spurs player since our trainer Cecil Poynton in 1928 to be sent off. A full-scale punch-up broke out at one stage and another of us was lucky not to be sent off when one of their players was left knocked out cold. Bobby Smith's elbows really could be lethal. We scraped through with ten men and won that tie by 2–1. Danny Blanchflower was back from injury for the second leg and he put me through to score our first in a 3–1 win at the Lane and we had done it. The first British club to reach a European cup final. The Double side were still pushing the barriers.

In the League, our form was becoming a bit patchy. Too patchy to win it, at least. For example, Bill Shankly's Liverpool side gave us a 5–2 drubbing at Anfield, yet only a few days later we walloped seven past them at White Hart Lane, with over half the tally coming from Jimmy Greaves. Desmond Hackett writing for the *Sunday Express* made me man of the match that day, writing:

> This was a Mackay Day. He wore his black suit of mud with the defiance of an Indian brave in all the majesty of his war paint. Once, when he was struck down in a bone-bruising tackle and lay writhing, the packed arena hushed. The fans knew that the indestructible Mackay must be sorely hurt. He rose limping. But as he moved into a chest-jutting gallop the roar of relief went up like a thundered prayer.

We only took one point from the last three matches and ended up as runners-up to Burnley. However, before the season was over we had beaten Atletico Madrid to win the European Cup-Winners' Cup. Sadly for me, I did not play in the final, having been suffering from a groin strain injury. This remains one of the few regrets of my career. I considered fibbing and telling Bill and Cecil that the strain I had picked up in training had mended itself, but knew that I was being selfish beyond the limit. There were no substitutes and had I pulled up, unable to run, I would have condemned Tottenham to a likely fatal disadvantage. I could not do it. Although I was delighted with the result and the performance, I could not hide my sadness about not being out there on the pitch with my pals. It sounds corny, but I was so happy for Tony Marchi, who had stepped in for me. Tony was a great player who had the personal misfortune of playing for a club at a time when they had one of the finest teams in all football history. At any other First Division side, he'd have been a regular – at Tottenham, he could not command a sustained first-team place. Being a part of that historic European victory must have been some compensation for him.

The match was played in Holland and there is a famous story about Bill Nick's pre-match talk. It is worth repeating because it is true and says much about the two men involved. Bill was running through the Spanish team, talking about their strengths and saying we should watch this and watch that. He was telling us how good his crosses were and how hard his colleague's shot was and so on. Eventually, Danny Blanchflower piped up and castigated Bill for building the other side up too much.

'We're every bit as good as they are, boss, and we will beat them.'

To Bill's credit he did not treat Danny's intervention as gross misconduct and allowed his captain to finish off the team talk on a high note.

The truth was Atletico were good. They were second only to the legendary Real Madrid in their league and were the holders of this particular trophy. But the lads gave one of Tottenham Hotspur's best ever performances and won the final in stunning style, 5–1. Greavsie and wee Dyson scored two each and the understated but ever-present John White got the other. They were brilliant, every single one of them, and it was Tottenham Hotspur at their skilful best. Jimmy Greaves says in his autobiography that he came over to me whilst the Cup was being paraded around the ground during the post-match celebrations and that he tried to comfort me, as I was not feeling a part of it. He remarks it was the only time he saw me cry. Cry I did, but I was feeling a cocktail of emotions that evening and the occasion had shaken and stirred them. Delirium at our success and disappointment at having not been a part of the climax.

We celebrated afterwards in Amsterdam and my emotional state had stabilised. I was out on the dance floor twisting with the best of them. Anyone who looked at me, as they undoubtedly would have, might not have believed I was in any way injured but that was the nature of my complaint. I could be perfectly all right and then if I tried to run, I'd be crippled. It was a good night and, today, if I hear 'Summer Holiday' by Cliff Richard or 'Please, Please Me' by The Beatles, I am reminded of that party. When I went to bed, I lay awake with a nagging sadness; a sadness that one feels at times of extreme happiness, a sadness that emanates from knowing that things may not be this good again. In my heart, I knew that the victory marked the beginning of the end of the Double side.

CHAPTER TEN

One Final, Two Broken Legs and a Funeral

Stanley Matthews pipped me to the Footballer of the Year award that season. I had come close a few times now and, having won the award in Scotland, I really wanted to win it. It would have crowned a great season and made some amends to me personally for not being able to play in the Cup-Winners' Cup final. I didn't begrudge Stan, but he was not the best player that season. He won it in recognition of his incredible longevity and his rejuvenation of Stoke City. At nearly 50 years old, there was no way he could have been the best player of the season. What they were giving him was a lifetime achievement award. Stanley had won the award before, as had Danny Blanchflower, and I believe that players should only be able to win once. Players' careers are so short and the opportunity to win the award so limited. Footballers such as Jimmy Greaves and Denis Law missed out whilst the likes of Stan and Danny won it twice.

At the end of the season, too, almost two years to the day since the shaming 9–3 defeat by England, I was recalled to the Scotland side. A few of us got the chop after that, understandably, in the hope of wiping the memory away, but slowly, as the wounds healed, one by one, we came back. Happily, the match I was recalled for was against England again and this time we managed to nick back some of our dignity by winning 2–1. Maybe the fact that my bogeyman, Johnny Haynes, was not playing had something to do with it, but we played well and the England side did include the likes of Bobby Moore and Charlton, plus my own teammates Maurice Norman, Jimmy Greaves and Bobby Smith.

I kept my place and was capped a further five times in 1963, but found myself out of favour again by the time 1964 came around. I assumed that, at the age of 30, my international career was over. A couple of matches against Austria in May 1963 stick in my mind for two reasons. First, the uncharacteristically filthy play by the Austrians at Hampden. We have come to expect brutal tactics from some South American sides, but I always thought of the Austrians as a gentle, non-violent race happy to wander around snow-covered mountains rounding up goats, but this night I could have sworn they were on a mission to mortally injure Denis Law. We had to really look out for him. Denis could well look after himself, of course, but with five or six maniacs chasing him around the field the odds were not good. The referee, Jim Finney, did not seem inclined to moderate the Austrians' behaviour.

Second, the team talk before the match in Vienna by manager Andy Beattie. He said he wanted Bobby Evans, the centre-half, to push forward and pick up their deep-lying centre-forward.

'I'm not doing that,' said Bobby. He refused point-blank and Andy gave in and changed the whole shape of the team he had outlined because of it. This may not sound remarkable now, but it was the first time I had witnessed a player openly and firmly not doing as he was told. Some footballers still called their managers sir; most of us used Mr, boss or guv'nor. Bobby's reaction was unheard of. Andy should have told Bobby that if he didn't like it, he was out of the team. He didn't and in my eyes he lost respect and authority from that moment on. I learnt an important lesson that day and one that would stand me in good stead later in my career.

The 1963–64 campaign got off to a good start as we won eight of the first ten games. No significant changes had been made to the squad. Terry Medwin had broken a leg during a tour of South Africa and was unlikely to play in the season and youngsters such as Phil Beal, Frank Saul and Derek Possee were challenging for first-team places, but that was the extent of it. Most of us had played together since 1959. However, one by one, we started to fall. I was the first.

The previous season's FA Cup winners, Manchester United, were our opponents in the first-round defence of the European Cup-Winners' Cup in December 1963. We beat them 2–0 at White Hart Lane, with goals from Terry Dyson and me, and we felt comfortable with that cushion when we travelled to Old Trafford for the second leg on 10 December. The date is carved in my mind and I can vividly remember all sorts of details even though it is over 40 years ago. The north-west of England was suddenly fashionable. Beatlemania had arrived and on the radio and television, and in the papers, you heard of little else. Another Liverpool group, Gerry and the Pacemakers, had been top of the pops with 'You'll Never Walk Alone' and Liverpool's home crowd, known as the Kop, had adopted it as their anthem. Their Scottish manager, Bill Shankly, who growled rather than spoke, was reviving the town's footballing fortunes spectacularly. All this was rubbing off on neighbouring Manchester as well and Matt Busby's new Manchester United team, which he had fashioned from the ashes of the Munich air crash, had the sympathy and second-team support of the nation. Soon the nation's spotlight would swing away from Liverpool and move to Manchester, where a young Belfast boy with a mop of black hair would make his debut for the United team. Once Charlton, Best and Law were in place, Matt had the best forward line ever in the history of our game. For opponents, that was an Englishman, an Irishman and a Scotsman story that was no joke.

United tore into us, utterly determined to make up the deficit and knock us out of the Cup. They were outplaying us, but I believe we would have held out if it was not for what happened to me. We were only eight minutes into the game when the ball was in their penalty box and I went charging in for it. From the other direction, their Irish defender Noel Cantwell was approaching with equal gusto. Commentators like to call these clashes 50/50 tackles – especially after someone has been hurt. I got to the ball and Cantwell got to my shin. I heard the crack and, if what people tell me to this day is true, so did half of the crowd. I did not feel any immediate pain, but felt immediate panic when I looked down and my foot had twisted round by 90 degrees. I really believed that if Cecil Poynton rolled down my sock and undid my bootlaces, we would find that my leg was detached. I was taken by stretcher into the dressing-room and can remember Denis Law being in there. He was really worried and sat with me until the ambulance came. Good old Denis. The ambulance men told me that there was a surgeon at the game and he was following in his car. It all started to become surreal after that. The surgeon took me into a room in the hospital and placed a transistor radio on the shelf as he set my break and plastered my leg. As I got woozy, I remember the game going into extra time. The surgeon would have been delighted because United won 4–1 and knocked us out 4–3 on aggregate. Of course, I was a little unhappy about having my shattered limb set by a United fan.

The surgeon told me that it had been a bad break and that it was possible I wouldn't play football again. I knew this only too well. Terry Medwin had been forced to retire after his leg-break.

After imparting this devastating news, he then asked what I wanted to do. One of the options he gave me was to return to the Manchester hotel where a reception was being held for both teams. I decided to do this and was driven across Manchester. By the time I got to the hotel, I decided to go straight to my room because by then I was hurting. Lads from both teams came up to see how I was, including Noel Cantwell. I was in no state by then to vent any anger. The next morning, I joined the team on the train back to London and remember sitting there with my leg resting on the seat opposite and playing cards. At St Pancras, Bobby Smith and Terry Dyson put me in a wheelchair and pushed me out to the taxi rank where we all got into a black cab and went back to my house. Only then did I start to pass out. The pain was indescribable. Isobel rang Bill Nicholson and he said that the Tottenham doctor would look at me the next day. Isobel said that was not good enough. An ambulance arrived and took me to hospital that very night and I didn't come out for six weeks. The first thing they had to do was reset the leg.

People refer to 'when I broke my leg'. As far as I am concerned, I did not break my leg. Intentionally or unintentionally, Noel Cantwell broke my leg. I don't think Cant (as I preferred to call him after that night) was anywhere near the ball. He may not have set out to break a bone, but that was the end result. I had a reputation as a 'hard man', but I was never a dirty player, and I would not have been able to live with myself if the situation had been reversed. I had ample time to think about all this as I lay in hospital. The London doctors had confirmed what my man in Manchester had told me: that the break was a bad one and there was a possibility that I may not play football again. I figured they were being gentle with me and the prognosis was worse than they were letting on. I decided that, if this break did put me out of the game, I would take revenge on Mr Cantwell. I couldn't make up my mind precisely how, but planning different strategies and methods of execution passed my immobile hours. I made no fuss at the time and even went along with the party line that the challenge was a 50/50 ball. I see Noel occasionally nowadays, at functions, and we smile, chat and laugh. We can do this because things panned out well. If they hadn't, we'd both feel very differently.

It would have been easy to become depressed, as I was aware that leg breaks often spell the end of a footballing career. I was pushing 30, after all. But the worried looks on the faces around me (including those of my family) just made me doubly resolved to recover, get fit and return to the Tottenham side. The biggest problem was my weight. Having a broken leg does not sate your appetite, but it does take away your ability to train and run off the pounds. I gained a couple of stone in no time and never again in my life would I get back to my pre-leg-break weight.

At the time of the United game, Danny Blanchflower had

played his last game for Spurs, although we did not know it immediately. That too was against Manchester United just before the Cup-Winners' Cup tie. Bill Nicholson dropped him and when he was not reinstated it became apparent that it was the end of the road for Danny. It was all left unsaid and at the end of the season, at the age of 37, Danny retired gracefully. He did not want to play in the lower leagues and, unlike most other footballers, he did have another career to turn to – his journalism. I asked him why he did not go into management. I felt that he had all the qualities that were needed: strong leadership, an absolute love of the game, a superb footballing brain and a thirst for further knowledge. I couldn't see how he could go wrong, but maybe he saw things I couldn't. I even suggested that he had a bit of a cheek analysing and criticising managers in print when he had not done it himself, but he laughed it off. It would be another decade before Danny decided to take the managerial plunge with Chelsea, but by that time he was past the peak of his powers and the game had changed radically.

Bill Nicholson had no choice but to start to rebuild and, typically, he bought carefully and wisely. Alan Mullery, a tenacious defender with a searing shot and bucket loads of drive, came from Fulham and Jimmy Robertson, a relatively unknown Scottish winger, was picked up from St Mirren. Both became fine players and contributed in spades to Bill's second great Spurs side. Compared with the team's recent successes, it was a poor season. Knocked out of the Cup-Winners' Cup and the FA Cup at the first hurdle was bad news and fourth position in the League was the worst showing since 1959. League form was erratic. As an example, we lost two games by 7–2, but won three others scoring six goals.

By the end of the season, my plaster was off and I was spending most of my time training and attempting to build up my leg. At first, it was half the size of the other one, but with the help of weightlifter Bill Watson we evened it up. I was hopeful that I'd be fully fit sometime at the beginning of the 1964–65 season. During the summer of 1964, Isobel and the children went up to stay with her parents at Whitecraig as she was ready to give birth to our second little girl and fourth child, Julie. She called me one evening and told me that John and Sandra White had called in on them whilst they were visiting John's folks nearby. They had their six-month-old son, Robbie, with them. She said that John was very excited because Bill Nicholson had given him a pay rise and told him he wanted to rebuild a new Tottenham side around him. Although I was pleased for John, I felt a pang of unease but reasoned I could hardly expect Bill to call me in and tell me that he was going to build a new Tottenham side around me when it was still not clear whether I would fully recover.

A few weeks later, in the late afternoon of 21 July 1964, I was sitting in the Viking, my favourite restaurant in Edmonton. I had eaten earlier and was having a drink or two whilst passing the time of day with David Williamson, a young lad who was trialing at Spurs, before driving back home. The phone rang and a member of staff took it. He called me over and said it was my pal Jimmy Burton from Dave Mackay Ties.

'Dave, have you heard?' His voice was flat and he spoke solemnly.

'Heard what?'

'Dave, John is dead. John White has been killed.'

Boomph.

I walked out of the restaurant in a trance and sat down in my car. I switched the radio on to hear the news, but a record was playing. It was 'It's Over' by Roy Orbison. I rested my forehead on the steering wheel and cried my eyes out.

I rang Isobel when I got home and she was distraught. That afternoon, she had received a knock on the door at her mother's house. A man introduced himself as a reporter and asked where John White's mother lived. Before she could ask why, the reporter enquired, 'How well did you know John White?'

'*Did*, why do you say *did*?' she said, feeling panic rise up in her stomach.

'There has been an accident,' replied the reporter, but then made his excuses and left.

Isobel switched on the television and there on the six o'clock news was the terrible headline that John had been struck by lightning as he sheltered from a storm under a tree at Crews Hill, our local golf club in Enfield.

John had gone to play golf with his best mate Cliff Jones. Cliff was late and John went out onto the first tee and hit a dozen balls or so. It started to rain and a thunderstorm developed, so John, conscious, I expect, that his clubs could conduct electricity, left his bag under one tree and ran to shelter himself under a large oak across the green. He was hit by a massive bolt of lightning and he was killed instantly. There was talk that his wedding ring may have conducted the electricity, but who knows? Who cares? All that mattered was that a lovely man with a lovely wife and young family had been tragically struck down. Literally.

Bill Nicholson and poor Sandra White had the unenviable task of identifying the body where it lay and they said it was an uncanny experience. They said it was like he was playing a prank, that any minute he would jump to his feet, grinning, and say 'Had you worried!' The next day, when we were all together, we could barely speak, any of us. I could not look at poor Cliff Jones because I knew if our eyes met we'd both start crying. They were so good together, Cliff and John. Great friends and always larking about. I remembered at one function how they had seen an ice-cream vendor's bike leaning up against a wall and they had rode it into the hall where we all were shouting out 'Ices, ices'. I thought of John's happiness on the evening that we won the Double when I asked him if he was glad he came down from Scotland. I thought of Sandra and the babies, and Sandra's dad Harry, and I thought of what Isobel had said about how excited he was about his future with Spurs. It was desperate. John was cremated at Enfield near where he died and the public lined the street outside. The newspapers, television and radio all reported on the service. It was a dignified and touching day as Britain said goodbye to an excellent footballer and, more importantly, a lovely, lovely young man.

Following John's death, the break-up of the Double side accelerated. Bill Brown lost his place in goal to John Hollowbread when he was injured, and when Bill signed a young Irish keeper from Newry called Pat Jennings, he could see the writing on the wall. Cyril Knowles was signed from Middlesbrough and he effectively replaced Peter Baker, who eventually joined Durban City and settled in South Africa. During the season, Alan Gilzean arrived from Dundee, where his club had won the League title.

By the end of 1964–65, a new Spurs side was in place. I thought it would have included me, but that was not to be. In September 1964, both Tottenham and I felt it was time for me to play in senior games again. I had been all right in training and practice matches, so Bill put me in a reserve-team fixture against Shrewsbury Town. I cannot tell you the name of the player who broke my leg this time because I have erased it from my memory. If I hadn't done this, it would have tortured me. I was holding up well when, as I stood like a stork on my left leg and played the ball with my right, the man came down on the back of my left leg and broke it again. I could not believe it. My first game back and crack! Utter bloody despair. Like Cantwell, this man did not get booked, let alone sent off.

A player can come back from a broken leg, but I cannot think of one that came back from two. Especially two breaks in quick succession and on the same leg at that. That thought was carried in everyone's head and showed on each face when they came to see me, although they did their best to comfort and cheer me up. For the first time, I had to consider that my career could be over. I had to fight any defeatist thoughts, though, and again vowed to think positively. I knew the drill and began the process of recovery straight away. Although I was ever present at the ground and at games, I was beginning to feel an outsider. There were now established first-team players I had never played alongside. Some of the youngsters only knew me with my leg in plaster. People round the ground felt sorry for me. Journalists came to the house and pictured my plastered leg on the coffee table and wrote stories with headlines like 'Iron Man says: I will return' and 'Anguish of Dave Mackay'. All this just made me so determined to come back because I knew that most people didn't think I would or could.

Tottenham did not have a great season. We went out of the FA Cup in the fifth round to Chelsea and slipped further in the League to sixth position. But the lads were still playing good football –

Bill Nicholson would not have it any other way – and most could see it was a period of transformation from one team to another. Jimmy Greaves was a constant and he still managed to put away 29 goals.

I threw everything into my recovery. I dieted furiously so I did not have to deal with losing the weight once I was back on two feet and I was careful not to rush into anything. When I came back, I did not want to be fretting over the slightest knock or wincing away from tackling. It took longer than the first break, but I was delighted when the doctors declared me fit for the new season. On 25 August 1965, I pulled on a Tottenham shirt for the first time since December 1963. We were at home to Leicester City and it was the most wonderful feeling. We were winning 4–0 until the final minutes when Leicester's Mike Stringfellow and Alan Sweeney pulled back two. The crowd made such a fuss of me and in the morning the newspapers did the same. The *Daily Telegraph* headlined with 'Spurs Give Leicester Severe Thrashing – Mackay The Master Is Great Inspriation'. This headline was the work of a kind sub-editor, I'm sure, wanting to lift and encourage me at this crucial time. I played a good game, but doubt if I was really man of the match. It may have been a pedestrian fixture, but that game ranks among the most special for me in my entire career.

Bill Nicholson boosted my confidence no end by congratulating me warmly and by telling me that he was making me club captain. It was the best thing he could have done. We won three out of the next four games and I scored two goals. It felt like old times and I immediately clicked with the likes of Cyril Knowles, Alan Mullery, Alan Gilzean and Jimmy Robertson. I felt Bill had purchased wisely and we would soon be challenging for the Championship once more. Back out on the pitch, I felt in control of my destiny for the first time in a while. My instinct to win was undiminished and I wanted to partner Bill Nick, as Danny had done, in the quest for perfection and entertainment on the field. Danny had continued effectively into his late 30s and I felt I had at least five good years ahead of me.

Jock Stein added to the comeback momentum by recalling me to the Scottish team for the match with Northern Ireland in October 1965. It was to be my final cap and we lost the game by 3–2, but I thank Jock for sealing my comeback by showing such confidence. Derek Dougan and the young George Best, by now causing tidal waves in the football world, were playing for the Irish. Both goalkeepers were my teammates – Bill Brown for Scotland and Pat Jennings for Northern Ireland. Another teammate, Alan Gilzean, snatched both our goals. Gilly was a great player, now often remembered for his glancing headers that seemed to be inch-perfect for foiling goalkeepers or landing at the hungry feet of Jimmy Greaves, but he was good on the ground, too. It was a great pleasure to watch the partnership between him and Jimmy grow and flower into one of the most effective in the First Division.

At the end of the 1965–66 season, we slipped back again in the League with an eighth-place finish. It was nevertheless respectable and Tottenham were generally agreed still to be playing highly entertaining football and posing a threat among the top teams. At White Hart Lane we certainly didn't feel we were in decline, just regrouping. Nobody, not even Tottenham fans, would have been overly concerned that summer about the domestic lot of any club because the World Cup was due to be staged in England and expectation was running high. Alf Ramsey, who had replaced Walter Winterbottom a couple of years earlier following his success with Ipswich Town, managed the national side. Another Tottenham connection in the England set-up was our own Jimmy Greaves in all his goal-scoring pomp up front.

As everyone knows, England won the World Cup, beating West Germany 4–2, and in the end Jimmy did not play in the historic final. I was sad for Jimmy; I had had a similar experience, although not as intense I suspect. I was lucky enough to be at Wembley on the day and it ranks as one of the best afternoons of my life. You could not help getting swept up in the euphoria of it all. I have never understood Scots who claim not to want to see England or any of the other home countries win. There is only one time when I do not wish to see England, Wales, Northern Ireland or the Republic of Ireland triumph, and that is when they are playing Scotland.

As the years have passed, there has been a school of thought that Ramsey's England teams played boring and negative football. I have never understood that either. The football played in 1966 and in Mexico in 1970 was among the best I have ever seen and, regardless of whether they won a World Cup or not, players like Bobby Charlton, Bobby Moore and Gordon Banks are among the players of the century. Nobody should ever detract from that fantastic achievement in 1966.

In November 1965, our big centre-half Maurice Norman suffered a broken leg in a friendly match. Like me, he fought to get fit again. He did manage to resume training after a long while, but I can recall sitting in the bath at White Hart Lane and Cliff Jones nudging me and nodding down towards his leg. Like the day my leg was broken for the first time, his foot pointed outward at a worrying angle. Also, when Maurice ran, you could detect a slight limp. Poor Mo never played competitive football again. There but for the grace of God went I.

Maurice was a big, lovable man and an integral part of the Double-winning side. I shall forever remember his long loping runs up the field to alarm all and sundry as he went forward for the corners. He was doing this when Jack Charlton was still at school studying for his coal-mining exams. Bill replaced Maurice with Mike England, a Welsh centre-half from Blackburn. As usual, it was a shrewd transfer by Bill, as Mike quickly established himself as the best centre-half in the Football League. Rarely did anyone disagree with that.

Bill had also recently signed Terry Venables from Chelsea. Terry had shown great promise in the midfield at Stamford Bridge and was a keen student of the game. He was not backwards in coming forward and his forthright views had led to some differences with my old landlord, Tommy Docherty, as manager of Chelsea. They were two men from a similar mould and, with hindsight, it was odds-on they would rub each other up the wrong way. There were no such problems between Terry and Bill, but we had a small run-in soon after Terry arrived. We were in the gym and I was adopting my favourite tactic of boxing a player in the corner and not allowing him to release the ball. Terry thought I was over the top one day and caught me with a cuff over my eye. He may have been wearing a signet ring (perhaps it had 'Tel' engraved on it) and it cut me a little. I returned a couple of blows to areas of the body that did not bruise so easily and we became the best of friends.

We entered 1966–67 more hopeful than we had been for some time. It was a team packed with internationals and boasted some of the best players of the era: Pat Jennings (Northern Ireland); Joe Kinnear (Republic of Ireland); Cyril Knowles, Alan Mullery, Frank Saul, Jimmy Greaves and Terry Venables (England); Mike England and Cliff Jones (Wales); Jimmy Robertson, Alan Gilzean and myself (Scotland). Now that Terry Dyson had moved on to Fulham and Ron Henry had packed up, Cliff and I were the only survivors of the Double side.

It was a vintage season and one where we played some of the best football in my time at Spurs. Although we were a very different team from the one at the turn of the decade and we would not enjoy as much success, for periods we were just as entertaining and just as exciting. Football basked in the afterglow of England's World Cup success and it seemed to raise everyone's game. Players with flair abounded wherever you looked and there were stars and idols at every club. I would argue there were more top-class players around during the second half of the 1960s than at any other time before or since and because of the rising popularity of televised football via *Match of the Day* and *Star Soccer* (later *The Big Match*) these players all became famous household names. There was McNab, McLintock, Radford and Georgie Armstrong at Arsenal; Trevor Francis and Bob Latchford at Birmingham; Willie Morgan and Andy Lockhead at Burnley; Charlie Cooke, Alan Hudson and Peter Osgood at Chelsea; Howard Kendall, Alan Ball and Colin Harvey at Everton; Tommy Smith, Peter Thompson and Ian St John at Liverpool; the European Cup heroes at Manchester United; Summerbee, Lee and Bell at Manchester City; Ron Davies at Southampton; Wynn Davies at Newcastle; Rodney Marsh at QPR; the World Cup trio at West Ham; and Derek Dougan and Dave Wagstaffe at Wolves. I could go on and on. Hundreds of players who on their own were worth the entrance fee to any game.

I haven't mentioned the Leeds boys in the above roll-call. They really were a great side with excellent players, but I think they spoilt themselves by playing very dirty football. It was all so unnecessary. With the likes of Terry Cooper, John Giles, Alan Clarke, Peter Lorimer and Eddie Gray in the side they were not short of talent and flair, but preferred to centre their tactics around snuffing other teams out with blunt and cynical tactics rather than merely outplaying them. In the first match of that 1966–67 season, we entertained them at White Hart Lane. Their terrier-like captain and fellow Scot Billy Bremner was my pal, but when he pulled his Leeds shirt on he seemed to become a different man and for some reason he kicked me on my newly healed bad leg. He was not going for the ball and he knew damned well what he was doing. He could easily have broken my leg for a third time. I was enraged. For a couple of seconds, I lost my rag and was temporarily capable of breaking his neck in return. I grabbed him by the front of his shirt and lifted him from the ground. Our faces almost touched as his legs dangled in the air. The moment passed, but not before photographer Monty Fresco had captured it on film.

The photograph has become one of the most familiar images of football from that era. I have certainly been asked to sign it many more times than any other image from my entire career and I have grown to dislike it. There I am, like Desperate Dan on steroids, manhandling a smaller and terrified-looking Bremner. It smacks of the bully. They say every picture tells a story and so does this image, but it is not the real one.

I was disappointed that when I was inducted into the Scottish Football Hall of Fame recently, they used this picture instead of one of the many other more positive images they could have chosen from. It has served to reinforce a perception of me in some quarters that I was a dirty player or, worse still, a bully. As I have said, I was never sent off in 30 years of playing football and neither Bill Nicholson nor Tommy Walker were managers who would entertain having a dirty and cynical player in their teams. It was not their style.

Myths grow, though, and, whatever you say or do, they take

hold. Not so long ago, Isobel and I were watching television late one night and a programme came on that we had not known about. It was called something like 'Britain's Dirtiest Footballers' and there I was, apparently number four on the list. I shared my 'honour' with the likes of 'Chopper' Harris, 'Razor' Ruddock, Norman 'Bites Yer Legs' Hunter and Vinnie 'Bites Yer Nose' Jones. Even though my playing career was by then three decades behind me, I went to bed that night quite hurt. I took some comfort in that the programme was on late, on a channel that few people watch or take too seriously.

I was also recently at Musselburgh races minding my own business when a man who introduced himself as an Everton supporter accosted me. 'I have to tell you, Dave,' he said, after asking me to autograph his race card, 'we've never forgiven you down at Goodison for ending Jimmy Husband's career. That was a bad tackle, that.'

'Were you there?' I retorted with anger rising up inside me, as I had heard this kind of thing before. There was no tackle. I remember the incident well and our bodies did not touch. Jimmy came running on my inside for a ball and I simply gave him a little three-foot hurdle by lifting my leg. He cleared it, but fell awkwardly and damaged his ligament. I know he was out for some time, but the fall did not end his career because I came across someone looking very much like Jimmy Husband at Luton a few years later. I haven't seen Jimmy since, but I would like to ask him if he really feels that I was responsible for his injury or for prematurely ending his career.

So good was our form that 1966–67 season, that right up until the final couple of weeks it seemed that Spurs could achieve the Double again. In the League, we only lost once between Christmas and the end of the year and we won nine out of our ten final games. This sizzling run of form was not enough, however, and we ended up four points behind the champions Manchester United. Nottingham Forest were second, with the same points as us, but they had a better goal difference. Had the season continued a couple of weeks longer, I believe we would have been champions. It was a shame not to be able to bring the title back to

White Hart Lane, but we did have the FA Cup final on the Saturday after the end of the season against London rivals Chelsea and we felt very, very confident.

The passage to the final was a fairly smooth one, but it was not without its moments. We drew Millwall in the third round at their notorious ground aptly named The Den. As Millwall had only just risen from the Fourth to the Second Division, and had never been in the First, I had never played on their pitch. I had visited their ground before, though, to watch my old pal Des Anderson, who was playing for them around that time. The match with us was one of their biggest games ever and an incredible 41,000 crammed into the little stadium. I mentioned earlier about the Roker Roar, well this Millwall crowd also had a way of helping their team win. It did not come in the way of singing or shouting, it just sort of hung in the air; a sort of 'go on, dare you, go and win' atmosphere. I remember, too, that it was at this game where fighting on the terraces first caught my eye. We drew 0–0 and only beat them by the single Gilzean goal in the replay.

Portsmouth, also from the Second Division, were our next opponents and we comfortably disposed of them at the Lane. Our charmed luck in the draw continued on to the fifth round where we landed Bristol City, also a Second Division side, at home again. I have stated before that I have never been sent off in my entire career and that is a fact that I am extremely proud of. Well, it is not quite true. I was once sent off, but I refused to go and it was in this game. Playing for Bristol was a guy called Johnny Quigley. I knew him because he had played for Nottingham Forest in their 1959 FA Cup final success and he also played when we put nine goals past them in 1962. I imagine it was that latter game that upset him. The referee had blown for a foul to Tottenham and Quigley picked up the ball. I ran over to take the ball from him for the kick but for some reason he decided to throw the ball smack on my nose. It hurt and my instinctive reaction was to whack him. Common sense said not. Instinct prevailed. He doubled up and toppled over, following a solid blow to his solar plexus. When I looked around, the referee was running towards me. His arm was outstretched. I pleaded and tried to tell him what had happened, but he was having none of it. I turned to Quigley, but he had made an amazing recovery and had sprinted to the box. I galloped after him and dragged him back to the bemused referee.

'Now, tell him what you did.'

Fair play to the man, he told him the truth. I thought that, if I was going, then I'd take this rascal with me, but it was even better than that – the ref ticked us both off and didn't even take our names. Oh, and we won 2–0. There were no hard feelings between Johnny and me, and I later met up with him when he was coaching in Kuwait and helped him get a position in Saudi Arabia.

In the quarter-finals, it was a Second Division club again. This time Birmingham City at St Andrews and I knew from experience this could be tough. We'd had a difficult tie with them in 1962 that went to a replay and it was always hard to beat them in front of their own very passionate supporters. Sure enough they held us to a goalless draw, but we well and truly walloped them back at our place 6–0. Now only the League runners-up Nottingham Forest stood between Wembley and us. The semi-final was a worthy tie between the second and third clubs in the League and goals from Jimmy Greaves and Frank Saul were enough to give us our victory.

Rarely can I recall such a fuss over an upcoming FA Cup final as there was between Chelsea and ourselves. Maybe it was just down London way, because it was remarkably the first final between two London clubs since the competition's inception. It was also an era thing. Chelsea Football Club were the swinging '60s personified on the football pitch. To borrow from the parlance of the day, the Kings Road was where it was at – and Chelsea FC were on the Kings Road. Fulham Road, actually, but who's arguing? Their players wore frilly shirts and bell-bottomed trousers. They grew their hair long and had grown things called sideburns. They may have been Mods and probably danced in places called discos to The Who and The Small Faces. Fashion models, photographers and film stars attended their matches. Over at Spurs, we still wore cardigans and slacks, sported short-back-and-sides haircuts and tapped our Hush Puppy shoes to Russ Conway tinkling away on his piano. You'd be more likely to find us at Walthamstow Dogs than Tramps or the Ad Lib club in the

West End. Yes, the media had this one down as a battle between the old and the new.

Chelsea had a good side, though, and we did not underestimate them. Managed by Tommy Docherty, there were two other Scots in the team whom I knew – dribbler extraordinaire Charlie Cooke and no-nonsense full-back Eddie McCreadie. Even more no-nonsense was Eddie's partner Ron 'Chopper' Harris, whose nickname gives some indication to his style of play. Up front they had Tommy Baldwin, Bobby Tambling and Tony Hateley, an old-style centre-forward who was lethal with his head. The jewel in their crown was Peter Osgood, a talented, skilful and entertaining centre-forward but, again, fortunately for us, he was recovering from a broken leg.

The record-buying public, and at the time that included most of us, would have bought Ray Davies' 'Waterloo Sunset' that week to propel it up the charts. The Chelsea hordes would have identified with Terry and Julie, the south London couple in the song. For Tottenham fans, loyalty may have persuaded them to buy the New Vaudeville Band's *Finchley Central,* but I doubt it. In my opinion, it was crap. The big news was the heavyweight boxing champion of the world, Cassius Clay, refusing to do his national service in America on the grounds of his opposition to the Vietnam War. A few weeks later, Clay would be handed out a prison sentence. He later re-emerged as Muhammad Ali.

We bossed the game from the off and Jimmy Robertson cracked in a goal to put us 1–0 up at half-time. Midway through the second half, I took a throw-in that I managed to chuck bang in the centre of Chelsea's penalty area and Jimmy again got on the end of it and tapped it into the path of Frank Saul, who hammered it home. We knew we were home and dry, although Chelsea's Tambling did snatch an unexpected consolation goal minutes before the final whistle, but it was too late.

I was proud of my throws. I always thought most teams wasted throw-ins and that they were not viewed as the set-pieces they could be. On the training ground, I practised and practised until I was able to throw almost from the halfway line into goal. It always baffled me why more teams didn't adopt this approach.

Ironically, Chelsea themselves did a couple of years later, when a boy called Ian Hutchinson broke into their team and he could throw. Really throw.

As I climbed the 39 steps to collect the FA Cup for the first time as captain and the third time in a Spurs shirt, I was extraordinarily contented. At 33 years of age, I had fought back from not one but two broken legs and had defied even my own inner fears of not playing again. I was not a sympathy case or in the team out of any misplaced nostalgia. I was in the team on merit and had captained them to the FA Cup and a great season generally. I felt as if I had achieved this not only for myself, but also for Bill Nicholson and all the Double Boys that had by then gone. I like to think Cliff and I had carried their spirit and ethos along and had imbued Bill's new young side with it. My only pang of regret that afternoon was for John White. This would have, should have, been his day too. Dear John.

I could not have wished for a better climax to my career at Tottenham. There's no topping this, I thought. But I didn't really examine the implications of that very accurate notion. I should have retired from playing there and then. It would have been the perfect end to a comeback from the footballing graveyard. But, like the boxer that has one fight too many, instead of hanging up my boots, I celebrated long into the night with the team, the manager and our families, and then relaxed at home on the Sunday and started to count down the days to the new season.

PART 3

Rams

CHAPTER ELEVEN

Baseball with Clough

Tottenham Hotspur did not carry their momentum through to the 1967–68 season. Whilst we did play brilliantly in some games, we lacked a consistency and I, for one, was conscious that my contribution was not as high as it once was. This made me unhappy and frustrated. I have recently read that Jimmy Greaves was nursing similar thoughts about himself at that time. We just weren't chiming. Early in the season, we lost 4–0 to arch rivals Arsenal at Highbury and this result was particularly hard for us and our fans to stomach. It was our worst defeat against them since 1959. Liverpool put us out of the FA Cup in the fifth round and we ended the season in seventh place. Before the final knockings, I decided to retire.

Our penultimate game was against Manchester City at White Hart Lane and the team which ended as League champions beat us 3–1. The scoreline was a flattering one for us: Mike Doyle, Alan Oakes, Colin Bell, Mike Summerbee, Franny Lee and co. made us look poor. As I traipsed off the pitch, I knew I was no longer good enough to play well in the top flight. Age and two broken legs had made me sluggish. I was one of the reasons why Tottenham were not as good and, if I had been manager, I would have dropped me and put me out to grass.

I went to see Bill Nicholson the following Monday and told him I was retiring. Bill seemed shocked and that shocked me. He said he thought I had a couple of seasons left in me and that, as far as he was concerned, my performances had been good ones. But I knew I was right and told Bill not to include me in his plans for the upcoming season. He shook my hand warmly and thanked me for my honesty. He asked that I not make any announcement or any final decision about where my future lay without talking to him first. I honoured that. The following Saturday, 11 May 1968, I pulled on a Spurs shirt for the final time against Wolverhampton Wanderers at Molineux. It was my last game and only Bill and I knew it. We lost 2–1.

I would have liked to have moved upstairs and become Bill's assistant, but his old playing colleague Eddie Bailey had filled the role vacated by Harry Evans' premature death. Eddie and Bill were a good team and, even if it was a possibility, I had no desire to rock any boats. Bill called me in to see him during the close season and I could tell by the smile on his face he had something he thought would delight me.

'I've been speaking to John Harvey at Hearts and they really want you back, Dave. They'd like you to be player–manager.'

My old mentor John Harvey had taken over as manager at Tynecastle following Tommy Walker's sacking two years earlier. It was an undignified end to Tommy's many years of excellent service to the club. Football clubs generally have a deplorable record in treating those who have given them great service. Since Hearts' Championship win in 1960, their form had been indifferent and mid-table finishes were now more the norm. John had no easy job, but it was typically bold of him to consider not only moving aside for me, but to actively court my return. Bill was right: the pull of moving back to my old club was a compelling one and I travelled to Edinburgh to talk to the club. Jimmy Wardhaugh, by then long retired as a player, bless him, met me at the airport. I'm sure the board sent him to stir up my feelings for the club and its history. Sadly, Jimmy died not so long afterwards.

The desire for a homecoming was strong, but there was one thing I was adamant about – I did not want to play football at Tynecastle again. Hopefully, I had left Hearts fans with good memories and I did not want to meddle with history.

I could imagine middle-aged men standing on the terraces, saying to their sons, 'See the fat guy out there huffing and puffing? He used to be Davie Mackay.'

Before Hearts and I could finalise any decision, fate intervened in the shape of a phone call at Dave Mackay Ties near the ground. 'Brian Clough on the phone for you, Davie.' How he traced me there, I don't know.

Brian Clough? I knew of him. Played against him once in a Scotland Under-23 match against England and my only memory was that he was sporting a massive shiner. I guessed he'd been the recipient of a defender's elbow in his Saturday League match. Other than reading that injury had cut short his career and a vague idea that he had gone into management, I knew nothing about him.

'Dave, Brian Clough here. I'll get straight to the point. I'm building a team at Derby County that will be in the First Division within two years and champions within five and I want you to lead it. Interested?'

It was a matter-of-fact, take-it-or-leave-it statement delivered in the soon-to-be-famous flat monotone voice.

'Yes, I'm interested to hear more,' I replied cautiously. 'Have you spoken to Bill Nicholson?'

'No, not yet. I wanted to ensure that you'd be interested before ringing Bill. I'll do it now. I'll arrange to come and see you in person. I think I can persuade you we're on the brink of something big at the Baseball Ground.'

I replaced the receiver and picked up a Sunday newspaper and scanned the end-of-season league tables. I finally found Derby County at 18th place in Division Two. He must be bonkers, I remember thinking.

He turned up a day or two later at the ground and we walked

out onto the pitch. It was a lovely summer's day and we sat down on the turf next to where the corner flag would have been. He looked fit and young in a neat suit, collar and tie, with his hair quiffed back almost in Teddy Boy style. He looked more like a trainee bank manager than a football manager. He was positively evangelical about Derby County.

'You would have heard about the goings-on at Derby?'

'Bits and pieces,' I lied.

He went on to tell me about how Derby was a sleeping giant and how, since his arrival at the beginning of the season just gone, crowds had jumped to 20,000. The board were fully behind him and funds had been made available for class players and the wages to pay them.

'You must have heard of our young centre-half McFarland?'

I hadn't.

'Well, I picked him up from Tranmere for peanuts. He's the next England centre-half. Jack Charlton's days are numbered. Mark my words. And I've signed O'Hare, a Scottish lad I coached at Sunderland. Brilliant player. We managed to get Alan Hinton, too. Great winger. England international. Now he's with us, we'll have him back in that England side, Ramsey or no Ramsey. And Kevin Hector. You must know all about Hector. The finest goalscorer in the Football League. You cannot stop that boy scoring goals for life nor money.'

I had heard of Kevin Hector. His name was familiar from reading the Fourth Division results, as he normally scored for Bradford Park Avenue (before they failed to get re-elected to the Football League) and seemed to have been around for years. Alan Hinton, too, was familiar to me from his time with Nottingham Forest. In fact, I had seen them all in action on the TV when they played and nearly beat Don Revie's mighty Leeds United in the semi-finals of the League Cup at the end of the season just gone. They registered with me and the country generally, but at the time it was not uncommon for Second and even Third Division sides to do well in that particular competition. Brian was still talking and systematically ran through all the other players as if they were all superstars and household names, and then he got on to me.

'I want you to be captain of my team. They will all look up to you and I think you can inspire them on to great things. I see you playing the role of sweeper behind the back four and controlling it all from there.'

His enthusiasm was infectious and his confidence shocking. What he said to me about playing as a sweeper appealed to me. Suddenly, I could see a few more years of playing football opening up. Danny Blanchflower once said footballers are a long time retired and he was dead right. Here I could carry on playing the game I loved into my dotage; Derby supporters didn't know me from Adam and therefore we owed each other nothing. If I failed and crumbled it would not happen under the microscope of Spurs or Hearts. Management could wait.

'Yes, Brian, I think I'd like to join you,' I heard myself say. For all of five seconds Brian Clough was speechless.

Football in Derby is as old as football itself. Even before the dancing men formed Hearts and the young cricketers spawned Tottenham Hotspur, football had been played in England for hundreds of years. It was a game played by boys and men, and entailed charging around the streets, lanes and fields with a piece of leather. It was an unruly and often violent free-for-all, and serious injuries, even deaths, were not uncommon. The keepers of the peace down the centuries attempted to outlaw it, but the tradition and will of ordinary people to let off steam was difficult to keep in check. A famous contest evolved between two parishes in Derby. It was fought out every Shrove Tuesday and Ash Wednesday, involving hundreds of participants and thousands more onlookers, up until the middle of the nineteenth century, when it was banned for safety reasons. It is from these battles between neighbouring sides that the term 'derby' or 'local derby' was coined.

Football games continued and Association Rules were drawn up in an effort to instil some order into the mêlée. A similar attempt to sanitise another sport enjoyed by the masses had taken place earlier, when the Marquis of Queensberry Rules had been introduced into prize-fighting. Schools and clubs adopted the

Association Rules first, and the game as we know it developed very fast between 1850 and 1880. Like everywhere else in the country, football teams sprung up all over Derby. Derby Midland and Derby Town were the two most successful, although they were soon rivalled by the football team formed by Derbyshire County Cricket Club, whose fortunes in the more genteel world of county cricket were at a low ebb. By the 1880s, Midland and Town had been absorbed by the more financially stable Cricket Club side and there was only one team for the town's football-bred and -hungry population to focus on. Derby County was up and running and already a founder member of the Football League.

At the same time, a local industrialist, Sir Francis Ley, was one of the area's largest employers, owning a thriving iron foundry business. He was unusual for the period in believing that he had a duty to supply his employees with recreation facilities, and he provided a large playing area for this purpose. In the 1880s, Sir Francis had visited America on business and had become very taken with the game of baseball. On his return, he became instrumental in setting up a baseball league in England and based his own Derby baseball team at the employees' recreation area. It soon became known as the Baseball Ground and, at the same time, Derby County Football Club moved from the County Ground to the Baseball Ground. Even though some of Derby's most famous footballers – including the legendary Steve Bloomer – doubled up as baseball players, the game never really caught the imagination over here and fizzled out. The last baseball game was played there during the Second World War, when American soldiers based in the area staged one final match. Football, however, was by then well established and thriving.

The Rams, as they were now known (probably as a reference to the sheep-farming industry which was prevalent in the countryside surrounding the industrial town of Derby), played their first game at the Baseball Ground in 1895 in front of 10,000 supporters. The aforementioned Steve Bloomer, already a hero at Derby and about to become an England international, scored both goals in a 2–0 victory.

Steve Bloomer is remarkable for being the only player who no living person could ever have seen play and of whom no film footage survives, yet who remains a revered name and is acknowledged as football's first superstar. He pre-dates even Derby County Football Club and as a boy would have been familiar with the old 'rough and tumble' football played on Shrove Tuesday and Ash Wednesday. Between 1892 and 1914, he played 525 times for Derby and scored an incredible 332 goals. In a short spell at Middlesbrough he played 130 times and managed 62 goals. Better still, he was capped by England 23 times and scored 28 goals. His name runs through the Derby County record books to this day: he is the only player to score six in a game; nobody else has matched his 18 hat-tricks; he was the oldest player (at almost 39 years old) to score a hat-trick and the oldest forward (at 40) to play for Derby. If it wasn't for the First World War, he'd probably have gone on longer.

During the Great War, Steve was incarcerated for four years in a German prisoner-of-war camp. When he returned, he turned out for the reserves for a while and then got involved on the coaching side before spending some successful years in Spain as manager to a League side. He spent the last years of his life back at home, poignantly sweeping the terraces and carrying out odd jobs at the ground he loved and that loved him. He died in 1938. When I arrived at Derby in the late 1960s, there were still plenty that remembered him and some who had seen him play. More than once, I heard an old gent in the crowd remark to a friend during a defeat, 'Steve Bloomer will be turning in his grave.' At the Baseball Ground, by the way, you really could hear what people said to one another, such was the proximity of the crowd to the pitch.

There are memorials, plaques and books about Steve Bloomer in existence today, as his legend has now been officially acknowledged by the club and by the town but, back then, when I first arrived, it was all word-of-mouth. Admirers of footballers around the turn of the century had no way other than the written and verbal word for recording a player's genius. The following poem, written about Steve, was adapted from a poem by Alfred Ollivant:

Bloomer is picked, and we will watch some more,
His carving swoop adown the field,
Amid old enemies, who yield
Room for his fleeting passage, to the roar
Of multitudes enraptured, who acclaim
Their country's hero bearing down on goal,
Instant of foot, deliberate of soul . . .
All's well with England; Steve is on his game.

During Steve Bloomer's time, Derby finished runners-up in the Football League once and made the FA Cup final and lost three times. In the 1920s, they bobbed up and down between Division One and Two, and did not find sustained success until the arrival of George Jobey as manager. Under his tenure, Derby boasted many talented players, including wingers Sammy Crooks and Dally Duncan, Jack Barker and Hughie Gallacher.

Gallacher was a hero in Scotland and had been part of the Scottish team that had thrashed England 5–1 at Wembley in 1928. It was England's first defeat at their proud new stadium, and that Scottish team was known thereafter as the 'Wembley Wizards'. It also included Jimmy McMullen and Hughie's boyhood pal Alex James, who became part of Arsenal's great 1930s team. Hughie was a 5 ft 5 in. ball of dynamite who scored goals wherever he went and fans of all of the clubs he graced hold him in great regard. He was, by all accounts, a quick-tempered and outspoken man who enjoyed his social life as much as his football. When Derby signed him from Chelsea, they were obliged to pay off debts that he had accumulated in London. Tragically, in 1957, when he was only in his early 50s, Hughie committed suicide by throwing himself in front of the Edinburgh–York express train.

In the seasons 1929–30 and 1935–36, Derby were runners-up in the First Division and, although being there or thereabouts, they still had not won a major honour since their inception. When the war ended in 1945, though, they found themselves with their strongest team in many years. It still included Sammy Crooks and Dally Duncan at the end of their careers, but the Rams had now acquired Jack Stamps, Peter Doherty and Raich Carter. Doherty and Carter were two of the biggest names in football. Doherty had won the Championship with Manchester City in 1937 and had a reputation in both his playing and character similar to the one that Danny Blanchflower acquired. He possessed a sharp and inquiring football brain, and could become frustrated with the people that ran the clubs and the game. Danny Blanchflower worshipped him and it was Peter, of course, who was Danny's manager when the two of them took Northern Ireland to the 1958 World Cup quarter-finals.

Raich Carter shared some of Peter Doherty's views on the administration of football. Like Peter, he too was a great forward and had won a League Championship and FA Cup medal at his home club of Sunderland. He was also unique in being the last (probably the first, too) player to boast the full Christian name of Horatio. Neither player was with Derby very long, but long enough to win the first post-war FA Cup in 1946. Raich and Peter scored 22 goals between them on the way to the final, where Charlton Athletic were beaten 4–1 in what is reputed to be one of the most entertaining FA Cup finals of all time.

Sadly, that team, many of them robbed of their best footballing years by the war, broke up soon after and Derby County entered a period of decline which, at their low point, saw them playing in the old Third Division North. In the late 1950s, they managed to scramble back into the Second Division, but never really looked like forcing themselves back into the First. The directors were not unambitious, though, and, determined to return the club to its past glories, they allowed Tim Ward, a former player, but by then manager, to purchase both Alan Durban from Cardiff City and Kevin Hector, the prolific goalscorer, from Bradford Park Avenue. In 1967, frustrated by the perceived lack of progress, they removed Tim Ward and brought in a young manager and his partner who had made noticeable progress in a short spell at the traditionally beleaguered club Hartlepool United.

Brian Clough was born in Middlesbrough in the north-east of England in 1935. Naturally, in that football-mad area of the country, he played the game from an early age and soon made an impact as a goal-scoring centre-forward that could talk the talk and walk the walk. He signed for his local side in 1952, but did not make his first-team debut in the Second Division until the relatively late age of 20 in 1955. Over the next six years, he scored an incredible 204 goals in 222 appearances. An astonishing goal-to-game ratio. In 1961, he was transferred across to neighbouring Sunderland, who were also playing in the Second Division. He was in his second successful season there, when, on Boxing Day of 1962, he sustained a knee injury that he never recovered from. Brian played his final League game in the 1964–65 season, before retiring at the age of 29. Even at Sunderland, he managed a goal tally of 63 in only 74 appearances. Despite his amazing goal record, and probably because he did not play in the First Division, Brian was only capped twice by his country.

Fired by a strong sense of being cheated in his playing career, Brian moved straight into management with Hartlepool United. It would have been difficult to have started any nearer the bottom of the pile. The only thing the north-east club ever won was the annual vote for re-election to the Football League. He persuaded Peter Taylor, a goalkeeper at Sunderland and a good pal, to join him as trainer and they set about stirring this sleeping minnow. In their first season, United finished 18th, in the second season they shot up to 8th and in the season after Clough and Taylor had left, United were promoted for the first time in their history. Before that, though, Len Shackleton, the old Sunderland legend, had nudged the Derby boardroom in the direction of Clough and Taylor as the management team that could lift their club out of Second Division mediocrity.

The Baseball Ground had the most unique atmosphere and, now that County have left it for Pride Park, it is one which will never be experienced again by a top-flight club. In contrast to Chelsea, for example, where in those days there was a running track between the crowd and the pitch, at Derby the spectators were close up to the touchline; as I said earlier, you could hear their conversations and feel their breath on your neck as you took throws. Players were more like fighting birds in a cock-pit than pampered superstars in a stadium. Some people didn't like it and worried about the crowd spilling onto the pitch (as they sometimes did), but I found it invigorating.

Brian's team of 'superstars' and future internationals didn't knock me out in my first few games for Derby. The drop in class was obvious (although welcome for me) and it wasn't until six games in that we recorded our first victory. I warmed quickly to my role playing behind the back three and felt that we were soon coming together as a side. The local population were also expecting something to happen, evidenced by the improving gates as the season developed.

In September, we started to hit form and I could see the players around me beginning to bloom. Young Roy McFarland just started to look better and better, and showed a maturity as a central defender far beyond his years. My other two closest colleagues on the field were full-backs John Robson and Ron Webster, and they didn't come more solid. As the season progressed, there was soon no better defensive team in our Division. Willie Carlin and Alan Durban were a spirited, tough and industrious midfield axis, and up-front I was soon wondering how Alan Hinton had been plying his trade outside the First Division. He was big and strong, with incredible speed and dexterity. When he set off on one of his runs down the wing, it was as thrilling as watching Nijinsky or any other thoroughbred racehorse turning Tattenham Corner in the Derby. In the middle, waiting for his feet-seeking-missile-like crosses was the fast-improving John O'Hare and Kevin Hector. Kevin reminded me of Greaves. He was a natural goalscorer – laid-back and lethal. Kevin just grew and grew in my estimation, although, perhaps because of his retiring nature, it took a long time for the football-watching public (outside of Derby) and his country to catch up on him. It was after a League Cup victory in October over First Division Chelsea, with their array of stars, that I realised Brian Clough was not a complete fantasist and that this team I had joined was becoming a bit special. Here we go again.

CHAPTER TWELVE

Players of the Year

I had never come across anyone quite like Brian Clough. You must remember my experience of managers up to this point had been confined to Tommy Walker at Hearts, Bill Nicholson at Spurs and, to a lesser extent, Matt Busby at Scotland. Tommy was a deeply religious man, who exuded inner and outer peace, and Bill and Matt were real gentleman of the old school. Although they could sometimes be cutting and resolute in their dealings with us players, they never verbally attacked people. Clough introduced me to a world of four-letter insults, slamming doors and even an underlying hint of physical violence. He was a whirlwind in the dressing-room. A man of extremes. Hostile one minute, almost loving the next. But his players adored him and respected him with a passion, and this was the key to his success. They were transfixed by his stunning self-belief and loyalty to them, and could see that he was changing their lives and their destiny. Some had been resigned to careers on the edges of stardom and futures played on grounds with names like Millmoor, Gresty Road and Gay Meadow. He was talking to them about *when* they were in the First Division, not *if*.

Peter Taylor was as important as Brian in the partnership. Peter went out and found the players, and he had an uncanny eye for undiscovered talent. Peter's job was to locate the players and deliver them to Brian. Brian's job was to ignite them. Peter identified good players. Brian made them great. It was perfect. They also worked the good cop–bad cop routine with the existing players very well. I would often sit there and watch Brian tear one of the lads to bits for a poor performance and leave him sitting there shattered and on the verge of tears. When Brian stormed out, Peter would slide along the bench beside the boy and build him right up again.

'He didn't mean that. He's just disappointed today because he has so much hope for you. He knows you can be the best person out there on that park and is upset because he thinks you've let yourself down. Don't worry. Brian adores you. You know that.'

I was never the object of Brian's wrath. He always treated me with nothing but respect and warmth. I think it may have been down to the fact that I was older than him and had achieved things in the game. He often said I was his manager out there on the pitch and, as such, I was regarded more as part of the management team than as one of the players. He would bring his two young sons into work during their school holidays and I would often play football with them. Simon and Nigel were smashing kids and, in later life, Brian has often said that I taught his boys to play. Not true, but very nice of him. Nigel grew up to emulate his father as a footballer and I have no doubt in time he will do the same as a manager.

Life was good and I was soon feeling very at home in the East Midlands. I lived at the Midland Hotel, just opposite Derby railway station and only a short walk from the Baseball Ground. I returned home on a Saturday after the game and then travelled back to the hotel on the Tuesday afternoon. Whilst it was not ideal being separated from Isobel and the children for most of the week, I loved the luxury of the hotel and it felt like home. When people came to visit, which they did most days, I'd arrange to meet them in the bar, or maybe the tea lounge or piano room. Roy McFarland and Jim Walker, two of our young players, were in digs around the corner and we knocked about together quite a bit. Jim, especially, was very fond of my Mercedes car and, as I had little use for it once I was ensconced in the hotel, he treated it almost as his own. One day, he came into training in a fit of giggles. 'Dave, you'll never guess what,' he said. 'I was speaking to one of my mates last night on the phone and he said "Jim, I saw Dave Mackay driving your car yesterday."'

Unlike some of my ex-colleagues at Spurs and in the First Division, I was not generally asked to do much in the way of advertising or endorsements. In fact, I was not asked to do any. George Best had his football boots, sausages and God knows what else, Gordon Banks had his gloves, Billy Wright pushed soap, Bobby Moore and Geoff Hurst did a Double Diamond beer TV advert and Dennis Compton plugged Brylcreem. Maybe the marketing people could not associate my looks and image with an appropriate product. Only when I got to Derby did I start to receive approaches. The first was from a hair care company who wanted me to be the public face of a hair-dye that claimed to hide grey hairs and 'take the years away'. Thanks, boys. I turned that one down. They'd be asking me to endorse stair lifts next – Thora Hird and I in a double act riding up and down the staircase. The one I did accept was from McEwans for Tartan Special. I never drank bitter in my life, but the money was good and all I had to do was grin with a foaming beer glass in my hand. It was embarrassing to see my ugly mug magnified many times on bill posters up and down the country as I drove around. Surely nobody ever decided to start drinking Tartan Special because I said I drank it?

Derby were looking after me very well financially. One of the directors told me 'off the record' that I was the highest-paid player at the club. I'm sure he told all the others the same. They also paid me well for a column I wrote in the programme and this was one of the reasons why the club were investigated for financial irregularities. It was never a secret that I was being paid for this, but I think there was some problem over how it was being accounted for in the books. Football managers over the last century have fallen foul of such investigations and, although there certainly has been some fraudulent activity, the bulk is down to ignorance of rules and regulations. Football managers are unlike any other managers. They have no financial training. They don't even have the advantage of managerial experience and a educational journey upward through an organisation. They are footballers one minute and managers the next, with the responsibility of assets, liabilities, budgets and all those other things that go with office.

On the pitch, I really felt that the Chelsea win in the League Cup was the turning point in our season. The precise moment when it actually turned would have been at 8.55 on the night of 2 October 1968. We had held them to a goalless draw at Stamford Bridge and got them back to the Baseball Ground. For the majority of the replay, we trailed to a Peter Houseman goal and then, in the 77th minute, I got on the end of a Willie Carlin back-heel and scored from 30 yards. In those dying minutes, we went into fifth gear and Alan Durban and Kevin Hector added a goal each for a decisive 3–1 victory. It was my first goal for County and I could not have wished for a more crucial one.

Next up were Everton, who were leading the First Division at the time, and would eventually finish third. Again, we held them to a goalless draw at Goodison Park before bringing them back to a hungry crowd at the Baseball Ground and beating them by a solitary Hector hit. This victory and second First Division scalp proved we were no fluke, and interest in the revival at Derby County was starting to catch the imagination of the national media. That Everton side was arguably their best ever, with the likes of Howard Kendall, Brian Labone, Colin Harvey and Joe Royle all playing at their peaks.

Swindon Town from the Third Division were our opponents in the quarter-finals and, on paper, we should have disposed of them with ease. But, as we had just proved, paper doesn't count for much in professional football knock-out competitions. It took a replay, but the West Country team of unknowns put us out in front of their success-starved supporters through a goal from their gifted winger Don Rogers. We took some consolation, I expect, in the fact that Swindon Town went on to win the League Cup, beating the mighty Arsenal in the final 3–1. Don Rogers, Rod

Thomas, Stan Harland, Frank Burrows and Peter Noble were no longer unknowns. Little did I know that these particular players would still be playing together a few years hence and would play an even more significant part in this eventful life of mine.

One day, Brian told us to expect his new signing from Hartlepool. 'McGovern is the boy's name. We had him at Hartlepool. He'll play for Scotland before he's 21.' That afternoon, a boy with fair hair and a neat side-parting arrived at the ground on a pushbike. As he approached us, I guessed he was a rather bold, adolescent autograph-hunter.

'Hello, I'm John McGovern,' he smiled. 'Is Mr Clough around?' When Brian appeared, he followed him off to his office. He'd follow Brian around for the rest of his playing career.

By Christmas, we were top of the Division, with Millwall, Middlesbrough and Crystal Palace snapping at our heels. In October, we had been 18th in the table. The rise was breathtaking and the best was yet to come. Of the eighteen games played in the 1969 section of the 1968–69 season, we won fourteen, drew two and lost two. We won the final nine games on the trot, with twenty-one goals scored and only two conceded! We were daunting. My style of play had changed, but I was pleased to see that the Football Writers' Association, as well as the Derby fans, still appreciated it. After a 3–2 win at Blackpool, *The Guardian* wrote:

> What a difference Mackay has made! From a middling, muddling, erratic team last season, Derby have been transformed by his experience. He bristles with authority, he shouts, he gets results from his younger colleagues. To see him pace his game, to recognise danger when none is clearly evident, and then, in averting that danger, spring his forwards into animated creativity, is a delight.

By the time we finished playing Millwall in our third-to-last game, we had won the Second Division title. By now, Palace were the only club that could catch us and only then by winning all of their remaining games. They slipped up. We eventually beat them into second place by seven clear points.

The scene was set for the last game of the season against Bristol City. It did not matter if we won or lost; 32,000 packed into the tiny ground to see us parade our silverware. Only two seasons earlier just 11,000 frustrated souls had turned up for the final game of the season. It was a fresh spring day, Concorde had just made its maiden flight, the Americans were about to land on the moon, the so-called summer of love had just begun and Derby County were back in the First Division. We tore Bristol apart; sometimes it was as if they were not there and, by half-time, Alan Durban had scored a hat-trick. Alan Hinton and Kevin Hector added to the tally in the second half. Alan Hinton also had a penalty saved and Roy McFarland hit the bar. If Sky were around then, and they had flashed up their possession graph, it would have read 95 per cent to 5 per cent. The real fun, though, was after the final whistle when we went up to receive the Championship trophy. An oil painting that captures the moment beautifully hangs in my bedroom at home: Brian Clough is shaking my hand as my other hand clasps the trophy; Peter Taylor is patting my back. The three of us are locked in a meeting of eyes that shine with mutual admiration. I love that painting and I loved that moment. Brian West, the artist, used a photograph to paint the picture and, as is often the case, the painting is far more evocative than the original photograph.

Of all my special days as a footballer, this day ranked as one of the most special. I think it was because it was so unexpected. A year before, I had sat in Bill Nicholson's office conscious that, although the mind was willing, the body was less so. I had told him that I wanted to leave White Hart Lane with my reputation and self-respect intact. Reluctantly, Bill had agreed and triggered the dialogue with Hearts. When I told him my decision was to join Brian Clough and Derby County, I could tell that he thought this was not the right move for me. My urge to carry on playing football for as long as I could overrode my plans to enter coaching or football management. I had figured that I could still be formidable in a middling team in a lower Division. Brian Clough's generous salary and three-year contract was a massive vote of confidence in my longevity and I had gone to the Baseball

Ground, if I am honest, hoping for no more than keeping Derby out of the old Third Division and looking maybe for a cup run or two to provide a high-profile swansong.

Instead, I was captain of a side that had won the Second Division in explosive style. A side that nobody expected would go straight back down and many agreed with Brian Clough that they would be challenging for the Championship in their first season. I was with a manager who was fast becoming one of the most famous people in Britain. I was relishing my return to the top flight and all thoughts of winding down had been temporarily banished. To cap it all, just after the season ended, I was named the Football Writers' Association Footballer of the Year. I remember marvelling at how life really is full of surprises and thinking to myself, life is good. So very, very good.

When I say I won Footballer of the Year, I actually won half of it. After years of being pipped at the post, when they finally gave it to me, I had to share it with Tony Book. Nothing against Tony but, if I win something, I like to win it properly. Tony had captained Manchester City to their FA Cup victory over Leicester City and his story was how Malcolm Allison had brought him into League football from Bath City at a relatively late age. Much was made of the fact that Tony and I had a combined age of over 70. I think the Association had made the decision that year to give the award to the old buggers and they didn't come much older than Tony and me. Tony's brother Kim, by the way, was a goalkeeper and had become entombed in football history for being the poor sod that kept goal for Northampton the day George Best scored six of the best.

In the close season, the club spent money on ground improvements that increased the capacity to over 40,000. Judging by the excitement in the town, they were going to need it. However, they didn't spend money on players and this was a great boost. Normally, when a club is promoted to the First Division – and these days the Premiership – players are purchased to aid in the step-up in class and to strengthen the squad. The message from Clough and Taylor was clear: you boys are good enough.

We started 1969–70 well, stringing together steady, but not

spectacular, wins. Our defence was solid. Our midfield and forwards were finding their feet against opposition more talented than that which they had been used to. By mid-September, after winning four consecutive games, Derby County were top of the Division. On the 20th day of that month, Tottenham Hotspur were our visitors. It was a poignant match for me. Nearly a decade on, nobody had survived from the Double side. Cliff Jones had been the last man standing, but he had been let go to Fulham. There were some new faces in the shape of Jimmy Pearce, John Pratt, Steve Perryman and Roger Morgan but Pat Jennings still loomed large in goal and Cyril Knowles, Mike England and Alan Mullery still bossed the defence. Greavsie and Gilly remained the attacking duo. Jimmy ran up to me on the pitch, smiling. 'Didn't think we'd be seeing you this quickly,' he quipped.

In that match, I witnessed Les Green, our goalkeeper, make the best save I have ever seen from a goalkeeper, and that includes the Gordon Banks gem in Mexico. Jimmy Greaves unleashed a fierce volley that looked like it would rip the back of the net out from fairly close in and Les Green dived and caught it almost effortlessly. He held the ball perfectly. It was like someone firing a rifle in your direction and you effortlessly catching the bullet.

The day we pulverised my old side by five goals to nothing, nearly 42,000 were watching. My teammates were making a fuss of me afterwards, believing that this victory must have meant a lot to me. But it did not. I was delighted we played so well and were making such an impact in the First Division, but I took no pleasure in the discomfort of my old pals and, as I had left Spurs with absolutely no acrimony, there was nothing to prove. Bill Nick, the gentleman as always, came and shook my hand after the game, but I was embarrassed for him. This had been Tottenham's worst defeat since losing to Burnley 7–2 way back at the beginning of my days with the club.

After Spurs, we beat Manchester United with Best, Charlton, Law et al., and then, as if running out of breath, we lost three of the four following matches, although we bounced back to beat Bill Shankly's Liverpool side 4–0. We were still in touch with the leading pack, but then followed a patch where we lost too many matches to be mounting a serious challenge for the Championship. If it wasn't for that mid-season slump, we could have won it because in February we beat Arsenal (who the following year would be the first club to win the League and FA Cup Double since Spurs) and then won seven of the nine remaining games. The other two were drawn. Our final position was a heady fourth and, with a quarter-final showing in the League Cup, where we lost after a replay to Manchester United, it was an excellent season. Brian Clough, Peter Taylor and Derby County had proved that we were no flash in anyone's pan and that we were dining at the top table.

Brian was also becoming a TV personality. He was outspoken and brash, in stark contrast to the more reserved managers of the period, like Alf Ramsey and Don Revie. Other managers of top clubs, like Harry Catterick at Everton or Bertie Mee at Arsenal, barely did any TV at all. Bill Shankly of Liverpool had charisma and the media seized upon his acerbic throwaway lines with relish, but even he was not one to linger around for the cameras. It wouldn't be long before Brian was doing the *Parkinson* show and had the honour of being impersonated by the leading impressionist of the era, Mike Yarwood.

The following season, 1970–71, promised much but delivered little. In hindsight, it can be seen as the period when Derby County realised they could not sustain a Championship challenge on the enthusiasm and the drive of Clough and Taylor alone. The squad had to be strengthened and class players added to replace the weaker or older players. One of whom was me.

I knew I was on the way out at the end of the season. I had signed a three-year deal and accepted it was unlikely that my contract would be extended. Brian was on record as saying many times that I could do what I wanted. That if I wished to carry on playing, I could, and if I wanted to hang up my boots, I could. But he was being polite. We both knew he had to make plans and that I would not be in them. When the popular Welshman Terry Hennessy was signed from Nottingham Forest in early 1970, it was no secret that he was my replacement. At £100,000, he was Derby's biggest signing. Earlier, Archie Gemmill had been picked up for £66,000 from Preston North End and turned out to be one of Clough and Taylor's most inspired signings. A Scottish midfielder, he really was a human dynamo who flowered under Brian and Peter to such an extent he became one of the best players in the country. He was one of the core group of footballers who followed Clough and Taylor wherever they went. Finally, Brian smashed his own record transfer by signing Colin Todd from Sunderland for £170,000. Colin was a natural successor to Bobby Moore in the England team. A gifted, fluent defender who played gracefully and, like Bobby, made it all look so easy. Alongside McFarland, there was no question in my mind that Derby County now clearly possessed the classiest defence in the country.

This was not a huge change in terms of numbers, but it was significant in terms of the shape of the team. We had a bad run between September and November when we did not win a game, but after that we picked up and only lost one of the last eight games, ending up in a respectable ninth place.

I was pragmatic about whatever should happen next. Brian Clough had given me three seasons of playing entertaining and rewarding football. Two of them at the highest level. They were three seasons I did not think I would have. I had been like a man with a failing heart being told that a transplant was possible and I could enjoy a further decade of full and active life. I had become acquainted and then emotionally attached to a third club and its people when I never thought I could or would. I loved those three clubs in equal measure, but for different reasons. It was all wonderful, but over.

I had no immediate plans, but had a strong feeling that something would turn up. I knew that I would go into management. It was not because of a lack of other opportunities; it really was something I wanted to do. There probably was a lack of other opportunities. I doubt if Lawrence McIntosh would have taken me back; I didn't fancy a pub in Edinburgh; it was a bit late now to ask Dad to get me on *The Scotsman*; and the thought of driving around the country trying to flog Dave Mackay Ties or selling insurance filled me with dread. I figured that one of my strengths was leadership – at least my managers thought so – and I had learnt a lot as a player and a great deal from those in charge at my previous clubs: Tommy Walker, Bill Nicholson, Brian Clough and Peter Taylor, as well as Matt Busby at Scotland. I was determined and prepared to graft. I was not on the Brian Clough scale of self-belief, but I was pretty confident I would make an impact as a manager.

Shortly before the end of the season, Brian called me into his office. I thought he was going to tell me I should retire and perhaps offer me a testimonial game. 'Swindon Town have come in for you,' he said. 'They've offered £30,000 and want you to play with a view to becoming player–manager.'

At first, I could not believe it. What good business. Derby County had paid Tottenham £5,000 for me. The low fee was in recognition of the fact that there was not a great deal of petrol left in the tank. Three years later, and at the age of 36, they were selling me on for a £25,000 profit. I could barely bloody walk, let alone play.

My final game as a player for Derby County was on 1 May 1971 at home to West Bromwich Albion in front of nearly 34,000. At the time, it was not definitely known this would be my last game, so it was not appropriate for the crowd to say goodbye to me and me to them. Shame. But there would be more adventures with Derby County to come.

CHAPTER THIRTEEN

Managing to Manage

Swindon were back down in the Second Division, but had spent much of their time since entering the Football League in 1920 in the Third and Fourth divisions. They didn't achieved greatness until 1968–69, when they shocked and delighted the country in equal measures by fighting their way to the League Cup final and beating First Division Arsenal. For a provincial Third Division side, this was some achievement, especially since it was coupled with them being promoted to the Second Division for the second time in their history.

The League Cup side had deservedly achieved God-like status in Swindon and they had been close to getting promoted to the First Division in 1969–70, but eventually finished fifth. However, in 1970–71 (the season that had just ended), they had slipped back down to 12th, as the League Cup momentum finally subsided. The board wanted me to join as a player with the intention of taking over as manager from Fred Ford at a later date. They were hoping we could do another Derby. It suited me because it meant I could continue playing for at least another season and that I would be setting out on my chosen road of club management at the same time. Swindon Town were the only club in Wiltshire and, with a large catchment area, there was the potential for reasonable crowds. Their fans had tasted success and wanted more. They may not have had huge financial clout, but I felt very confident that I could contribute to steadily improving their situation.

I set up in my new home – the Blunden House Hotel in Swindon – and adopted the same work–home pattern that had worked at Derby. I would miss the Midland Hotel. I met the players and did my best to dispel any negative feeling about my coming. Being a manager-in-waiting can be a difficult position. Not only for me, but for the manager and for the players, who are not sure whether to relate to me as a teammate or as their future boss. The team was basically the same one that had beaten Arsenal and I was a bit surprised that the club had not used the money made from their Cup run and improved crowds to invest in some new players. They were not a particularly young side and that was the first thing I noticed. At Derby, I was surrounded by youngsters who did much of the work for me and allowed my tired legs to take it that much easier. At Swindon, the average age was older than that at Derby and they were not about to run themselves ragged for poor old me.

There were some good players at the club. Rod Thomas, whom I mentioned before when he impressed me in a match against Derby, was a classy defender and I was surprised that he had not yet been picked up by a First Division club. Frank Burrows and Stan Harland were strong, solid, reliable players, providing valuable leadership and steel in the defence. Peter Noble was an industrious and skilful midfielder who I also believed was capable of playing at the highest level, and Don Rogers was a pleasure to see in action. He had scored two of the goals in the historic Arsenal victory and was a winger with extraordinary pace who loved to cut in and swivel past players then go for goal. He scored more goals than the average wing-man. There were two schools of thought about Don. One was that he was great at Swindon but would not be able to shine against First Division defences; the other was that he was so good he should play for England. I subscribed to the latter; however this would not happen with Alf Ramsey in charge, given his aversion to old-fashioned flank men.

I believed that Swindon Town could be taken on to better things if a side was built around these and a couple of other lads, but new and young blood would have to be introduced and, sadly, in order to be able to raise the money to do this, Rod, Peter or Don might have to be sold. I sensed straight away that the fans were averse to any of the League Cup-winning side being sold. This was admirably loyal, but impractical.

In November 1971, Fred Ford resigned. His position had been made untenable, but not by me. The Swindon board had approached me in the first place. Fred had taken over from Danny Williams, who had led Swindon to promotion and the League Cup success but then taken a bigger job at Sheffield Wednesday, and Fred had done well. In his first season, he guided them to fifth position in Division Two and to winning two Anglo-Italian tournaments, but in his second season they finished mid-table. This is when they asked me to join and gave me the impression it was a smooth and agreed succession. I thought the board were being premature in getting rid of Fred; halfway was hardly disastrous. But boards are like that. When I arrived and realised that Fred may have not been totally in the picture (or the one that had been painted to me), I refused to step into his shoes until Fred's contract was up. As this had some time to run, I imagine Fred felt tremendous pressure from the board to step aside. It was a shambles and typical of the way many managers are treated in the game, and explains why they can sometimes seem to act disloyally. They soon learn that loyalty, patience and decency are qualities that are often lacking in their employers.

Still, I had my start to make as a manager and had been hired to do a job. It would not be good on my CV to start falling out with directors before I had even sat behind a desk, so I just got on with it. Our season ended marginally better than the previous one, with an 11th-place finish. I had not disgraced myself, but I had not set the world alight. I was reasonably satisfied, though, as I was only six months into my managerial career. The ship was steady and I knew I now needed to assert my authority, stick my neck out and start to make things happen. I employed Des Anderson, my old chum from Edinburgh and ex-Millwall player, as my assistant and immediately sent him out on the prowl looking for undiscovered talent. There was no money, but I was determined that should not be an insurmountable barrier to our success.

What I did next probably did not help me in the popularity stakes. When Birmingham offered £15,000 for Stan Harland, I accepted. To me, it was good business. Stan was in his early 30s, past his best, and that sort of money for a defender of that age was not bad. To the fans, it was a betrayal and a flawed decision. They were right and I was wrong on one count at least because Stan played some great football at Birmingham City and helped power them back into the First Division.

My last ever competitive game as a player was on 1 April 1972, when we drew with Portsmouth 2–2 at Fratton Park. I'd put myself on as a substitute when we were 2–0 down with 15 minutes to go. When I had made my Scottish League debut in November 1953, Winston Churchill was the Prime Minister, Queen Elizabeth II had just been crowned, people still wore demob suits and carried ration cards, and you were the business if you drove around in one of the new Austin Sevens. Einstein was still alive, for God's sake. Now Ted Heath was Prime Minister, Churchill was long dead, young people walked around with glitter on their faces and bounced along in stack-heeled shoes with manes of curly, permed hair. The car to have was the sleek Ford Capri. Put next to the Austin Seven, you'd have thought that motoring had entered the space age. Footballers no longer worked down coal mines; indeed, soon nobody at all would be working down coal mines. The maximim wage for footballers was a distant memory and some were even now becoming wealthy. It was a different world.

That close season of 1971–72 was a reflective one for me. The team I had just left, Derby County, had won the League. Colin Todd was wearing my shirt but, other than that, it was more or less the same players that Brian and Peter did it with. It was a tremendous achievement in just a few years to emerge from Second Division obscurity to champions and playing in Europe.

Clough had done everything he said he would. People had to believe him now, whether they liked it or not. His personal stock could not have been higher. From player to manager, from manager to celebrity, and from celebrity to God. It is easy to forget just how big he was during that period. He had performed a miracle and, in a country that was ravaged by industrial strikes and plagued by power cuts and three-day working weeks, the country's eyes rested on him for a while, wondering. I have no doubt that, had Brian decided to stand as an MP, especially in Derby, he'd have won by a landslide. He had strong views on just about *everything* and must have been tempted. I was delighted for Derby County and, of course, I was a little bit jealous and a little bit sad that I couldn't have held on just that little bit longer at the Baseball Ground.

At the same time, Tottenham Hotspur were coming good again, finishing sixth in the League and winning the UEFA Cup by beating Wolverhampton Wanderers in a tonsil-burning two-leg final. On the way there, they had seen off Rapid Bucharest and AC Milan. I was so glad for Bill Nicholson and Alan Mullery, Joe Kinnear, Cyril Knowles, Mike England, Phil Beal and Alan Gilzean, who all survived from my time at the club. It was a deserved reward for Bill and his ongoing commitment to playing entertaining, flowing football come what may. Jimmy Greaves had by then retired after leaving Spurs and spending a short time at West Ham. Although it was not generally known, Jimmy had developed a drink problem. When it finally hit the papers, I was dumbfounded. Although I had drunk with Jimmy on numerous occasions, especially in the Bell and Hare, I never saw him under pressure through drink. His imbibing habits were no worse than any of us, as far as I could see. He called me 'King of the Bar Stool' and considered me to be the leader of the Tottenham Players Drinking Club, not the other way around. All I can think is that when we finally sloped off home to bed, he carried on in some other place.

The great success of my former clubs brought my position into sharp focus. They were the toast of the media and their communities, but I was in a footballing backwater struggling to learn a new trade at a club with little money and fans who had no reason yet to bestow any automatic affection or respect on me. It was a lonely position for a man who had been used to being at the centre of Planet Football over the previous 20 years.

In October 1972, just one year after taking over at Swindon, I was approached by Nottingham Forest and offered the post of manager. It was an offer I could have refused, but didn't. Forest were doing only a little better than Swindon in Division Two, but they were a big club with a long and rich history, and only ten years earlier had been one of the top clubs in the country. We entertained them at the County Ground and drew 2–2 in late October, and it was at that game that one of the Forest directors sounded me out. At Swindon, progress was slow and my whole future was finely balanced. If I did not improve Swindon's lot significantly, I would be deemed a failure. Worse still, if Swindon slipped under me, I *would* be a failure. Few managers have survived relegation in their first post. Only managers with a long and well-known track record can come back from failure. I feared that could happen to me and that my managerial career would be over before it started. I did not like the thought of leaving a job unfinished and I honestly believe that I would have managed a steady improvement at the club, but with the absence of funds it would be a long, tortuous process. In real life, you make the decision that is best for you and yours. A few months later, clubs like Forest might not have been interested in securing my as-yet unproven talents as a manager. I don't know if too many tears were shed over my resignation as Swindon manager; some were glad to see the back of me, especially after I sold Don Rogers to Crystal Palace for £170,000. Don, by the way, enjoyed further golden years at Palace and very nearly did force his way into the England team.

Nottingham Forest had only just dropped into the Second Division, following a good decade and a half in the top flight. As recently as 1967 they had finished runners-up in the League. However, by the time the club approached me, instead of bouncing straight back into the First Division, they looked like they might struggle, and this fear cost manager Matt Gillies his job. They were a big club with a determination to revive their fortunes; there was money available and good cash-flow-generating crowds. I was immediately impressed with the players, both established and coming through the ranks. I really felt that Des Anderson and I were on to something big. Martin O'Neill and Duncan McKenzie were impressive – both would become household names – and Tony Woodcock, John Robertson and Viv Anderson were all youngsters pushing into the team.

My first game in charge was at home to Millwall in November 1972 and we won 3–2. The City Ground crowd gave me a warm welcome and I was soon convinced that the move I had made was the correct one. However, the going got immediately tougher when we lost our following three matches and slipped to fifteenth in the table. The directors were supportive, though, and indicated to me that I had time to rebuild and improve the side and, barring relegation, they would give me that time. Of course, half-communicated assurances like that mean little in football, but I didn't feel that I was having to look over my shoulder too much in those first days. We steadied our form and there were promising signs of a good team forming. Although we finished 14th at the end of the season, the supporters recognised that the team was improving.

We went into 1973–74 buoyant and opened well. The team was starting to mesh together nicely. The youngsters we were bringing through were looking good. A quarter of the way through the season we were in third position and promotion was looking very possible. I was very happy at Forest and my relations with the board, the players and the fans were good. I was not interested in moving on. The Mackay family had moved house to Burton Joyce in the close season, a delightful village just a few miles outside of central Nottingham, and we remain there today. I knew that I had to prove myself there and I was determined to do so. If someone had asked me on Saturday, 13 October, after we had lost in a League match at Orient, if I could see any circumstances in which I would voluntarily leave Forest, I would have replied that, barring some earth-shattering developments at Spurs or Derby, and I was for some reason offered the job there, my answer would be no.

On 15 October 1973, however, an earth-shattering development did take place down the road at the Baseball Ground. Brian Clough and Peter Taylor resigned from Derby County and the biggest soap opera in football to date started to unfold.

Seemingly, the board at Derby had become increasingly uncomfortable with Brian's celebrity status and his outspoken comments about the game and anything else chucked at him by delighted journalists. Brian had also recently accepted a job with London Weekend Television to lead ITV's football coverage in place of the departing Jimmy Hill, who was moving over to BBC's *Match of the Day*.

Brian had become very powerful and there is one thing that powerful men, like the owners of football clubs and companies, do not like and that is other powerful men. They felt that Brian Clough thought he was bigger than the club. Brian knew he was. Brian resigned on behalf of himself and Peter after one of the directors had questioned Peter Taylor, very insultingly, as to just what his role was at the club. Once this was out, the press descended on the Baseball Ground in their droves and all the news bulletins were dominated by the unfolding events at Derby County. The saga even usurped the Yom Kippur War and the burgeoning Watergate scandal from the front pages of the national press as each new development built the momentum. The club were investigating Brian over irregularities; Brian was suing the club for slander; the fans were protesting; the players were going on strike. Football had never witnessed anything like it. Like the rest of the country, I was transfixed. It was one of those times when you really did not know what would happen next. For a few days, it was finely balanced. Brian Clough, on a wave of people power, looked like he just might unseat the entire board of the company that paid his wages and in which he did not own one single share. I had sympathies with both sides – I liked and admired Brian and likewise the chairman, Sam Longson, a down-to-earth millionaire who had been nothing but fair and honest with me. I knew exactly what he wanted when I saw him walking towards me that day in

October 1973 in the near empty boardroom at Northampton Football Club, when I was up there watching Forest reserves.

He said I was the only man in the country who could replace Brian Clough as manager of Derby County Football Club and he was right. I was under no illusions. I knew I was only being offered the post because there was no other person who might be able to unite the players, fans and board behind the club in the midst of this mass revolt. I had achieved nothing in management yet and, although the start at Forest was promising and my time at Swindon by no means a failure, I still had it all to prove. I didn't have to think long about the offer. You either see the glass half-full or the glass half-empty. I see it as half-full and then drink it. Derby County in October 1973 could have been viewed equally as a marvellous opportunity for a young manager or a poisoned chalice.

I was not happy about leaving Forest, but I knew Derby County and this job was my destiny. I could never have dreamt I would have got to that particular hot seat so quickly, but life has a habit of surprising everyone. When I had taken over Forest, they were sixth or seventh from bottom and relegation was a real fear. That's why they were looking for a new manager, after all. I left them a year later sixth or seventh from the top with promotion a real possibility and the foundations of a good side. I had signed a lad called Ian Bowyer from Leyton Orient and felt that he would go on to great things. Nevertheless, I was leaving a job unfinished, and the fans and the club had a right not to be too happy with me. I saw those feelings close up after my last home game in charge, when it was well known I was about to leave for Derby. Angry fans had gathered in the car park at the City Ground and were making threatening noises. One of the directors advised me not to go outside and I didn't until the crowd had dispersed.

Managers have to capitalise on their purple patches in this game of ours. You can lose three games on the trot and find yourself in the dole queue, even if you have won honours the previous season. The pressure on managers to perform can be intolerable. Club chairmen possess short memories and very few of them can plan for the medium term let alone the long term. A manager knows his job is only as safe as his previous few results and, therefore, to expect absolute club loyalty is unreasonable. That was then. It's worse now.

The fracas at Derby was not subsiding. I knew how serious it was when Roy McFarland, then captain of the County team, rang me at home and advised me not to come.

'Dave, we've got every respect for you,' he said, 'and you're our pal, but please don't come. It's not fair on you. We want to get Brian back and I think we will.'

'I've accepted the job, Roy. Simple as that. Brian's not coming back and, if you don't get me, you'll end up with someone else.'

Roy was not convinced. Then Henry Newton rang. Brian had only just signed him from Everton. He said much the same thing and I gave him the same message.

I read in the papers that Derby had offered the job to Bobby Robson initially. Bobby was riding high with Ipswich Town, who were enjoying their finest years since Alf Ramsey had elevated them a decade earlier. If the press are to be believed, he rejected Derby because he felt nobody could follow Brian. Reading the press generally was stressful. Brian Clough v. Sam Longson was being fought out on their pages. The pro-Brian camp (which included almost every newspaper) was doing its best to undermine me before I had even started. The players were quoted as saying they would not play for Dave Mackay and that they were not going to attend training and would effectively go on strike. Brian was supposedly meeting them in hotels and guiding their every move. Some of it was obviously nonsense, but still most unsettling.

On my first day as manager, I drove into the tiny car park at the Baseball Ground and squeezed in between two cars. As I put my handbrake on, a small crowd of protestors surrounded my car and one banged with his fist on the windscreen.

'Fuck off, Mackay. You're not welcome here,' he snarled.

Now, I don't mind people shouting and swearing at me, but attempting to damage my car or laying hands on me is a different matter. I growled and jumped out of the car and went for him. He ran very fast out of the car park.

'Who was that man?' I asked the other banner-carrying fans.

'Tell him to come for a trial. I think we could use him on the wing.'

Some of the protestors almost smiled.

I had decided not to allow the whole Clough thing to divert me and rather hoped that when Mike Bamber, chairman at Brighton & Hove Albion, appointed him as manager that the whole thing would fizzle out. Sadly not. I gathered the players together and said much the same to them as I had to Roy and Henry over the phone. Brian wasn't coming back. If it is not going to be me, it will be someone else. Someone you may welcome even less and, if you still don't like it, you should table a transfer request because we have a job to be getting on with. Nobody rushed up and hugged me, but then again nobody walked.

The roughest ride of my professional life was to follow. We lost the first three games of my tenure, scored only once and conceded eight. Before I knew where I was, it was getting towards Christmas and we still had not registered one victory with me as manager. We had tumbled from third position down to fifteenth. The BBC were highly critical of me (the BBC being the 'Bring Back Clough' campaign that was still gripping the town). BBC was daubed on walls around the ground and town, and cars drove around with BBC stickers on their rear windscreens. I liked to draw up level with such cars in traffic and turn sideways and smile broadly at the driver and flash some manic eyes. The BBC stood outside the office every day and at games, handing out leaflets which amplified Derby's performance under me. As if anyone did not know. Fun, it was not. On 15 December, we travelled to St James's Park to play Newcastle United. The spirit on the coach was depressed. I sat at the front, putting a brave face on the situation, but knowing I was now between 90 and 180 minutes of football away from the sack and a likely end to my managerial career. The tone in newspaper articles betrayed the opinion that I was Derby's ex-manager in waiting, destined to be a footnote in managerial history as the poor sod that tried to follow Brian Clough.

Newcastle slaughtered us that day and we deserved to lose four or five nothing, only the woodwork prevented it. Somehow, two goals from Alan Hinton and Roger Davies against the run of play gave us the victory. Luck was with us. On the coach coming back, we listened to the draw for the FA Cup third round and a cheer went up when we heard we'd got non-League Boston United. The players were smiling. I felt the pressure lift just a little. That was the turning point.

Alan Hinton did it again the next week when he scored the two goals that gave us a victory over my old club Spurs and we then continued a good vein of form for the rest of the season. We ended in third position and finally the BBC campaign began to switch off. I had added to the squad by entering the transfer market for the first time in my career in a significant way and signed Rod Thomas, the Welsh full-back from Swindon who had impressed me so, and Bruce Rioch from Aston Villa for £200,000. Bruce was a tough, attacking Scottish midfielder who could open up defences like prising open a tin of corned beef, with surging runs and goals scored with his power-driver of a shot. I thought he was among the best players in the game and was sure that £200,000 would prove to be a snip.

In the close season, I heard that Franny Lee was up for sale at Manchester City. I loved Franny as a goal-scoring, bustling centre-forward and he had always given me grief when I was a defender. He had won almost everything with City, including the League, the FA Cup and the European Cup-Winners' Cup, and had been a regular in the England team. Now he was 30 years of age, the considered opinion was he was past his sell-by date. Nonsense. One man's 30 is another's 26. I was very happy to pay £100,000 for him. Franny was his own man, with burgeoning business interests outside the game, and was equally of the opinion that he still had plenty to give. He said yes and was soon occupying my old room at the Midland Hotel.

Sadly, Roy McFarland, the linchpin of our side and already a young veteran at Derby, got injured in an England match at Wembley in May and was to be out for most of the coming season. Up until then, our defensive trio of David Nish, Colin Todd and Roy had also been the axle of England's defence. Peter Daniel, a loyal servant of Derby, who had been in and out of the first team since 1965, stepped up to take Roy's place. He was to enjoy his finest hour. The side that started and finished the 1974–75 season normally included: Colin Boulton in goal, Ron Webster, David Nish, Colin Todd and Peter Daniel in defence, Bruce Rioch, Henry Newton and Archie Gemmill in the middle of the field and Roger Davies, Kevin Hector, Franny Lee and Alan Hinton up-front. Ron Webster had been playing solidly for Derby even longer than Peter Daniel and only when he was injured during the season did he lose his place to Rod Thomas.

We started off steadily with a couple of draws, but improved with every game. After Christmas, we steamed ahead, along with Liverpool and Ipswich, and the prospect of Derby winning a second Championship was a real one. We were playing great football with some emphatic wins. Rioch was electric and finished the season as our top scorer, despite being a midfield player, with 15 goals. Kevin Hector, Roger Davies and Franny Lee were close behind with 12 each. Everyone was up for it. There was not a weak link. The board, most of them anyway, were happy and so were the supporters. It was a great time.

We had a great run-in to the end of the season, winning six out of seven games, the last two being against West Ham and Wolves. We also battled through to the quarter-finals of the FA Cup and the third round of the UEFA Cup, in which we beat Atletico Madrid, but went out in the following round. Our penultimate League game was a draw against Leicester. We were top of the table with fifty-two points with one game left against already relegated Carlisle at home. It looked like the Championship was ours. During the week, we had a reception at Bailey's nightclub to celebrate Peter Daniel being voted Derby County Player of the Year. Ipswich Town were playing Manchester City that evening and they had to win to have a chance of catching us, and then only if we slipped up against Carlisle. I was trying to stay calm as the speeches and the meal progressed. Barry Eccleston of Radio Derby was dining with us and had a transistor radio with an earplug wired up to him, and he was making faces and signs to me across the table about the progress of the Ipswich and City match. I could only nibble at my prawn cocktail.

Finally, he ripped the plug from his ear and announced, 'It's a draw. A bloody draw. We're champions!'

A huge cheer went up and we all embraced our wives and each other. A round of applause started and what began as a celebration for Peter Daniel turned into a huge party for everyone. I loosened my bow tie and accepted a glass of champagne. A huge sense of relief and achievement swept over me and I was ecstatic. For the first time, I did not feel the hand of Brian Clough on my shoulder. I felt vindicated and a sense of enormous personal satisfaction. I felt great admiration for the players. All of them. They had put the trauma of 18 months earlier behind them, gelled with new players and proved they were again the best side in the country. I was especially happy for Franny, who would not have placed a bet on himself ever playing in another Championship side. For Peter Daniel, also, who had stepped out of the shadows and performed brilliantly, and for Bruce Rioch, who added such impetus. For Roger Davies, who sometimes got stick for looking clumsy, but astounded TV viewers in a match against Luton when he scored all five goals. For Kevin Hector, for keeping his head down and just getting on with it. For Archie Gemmill, for covering every blade of grass in the First Division. For Colins Todd and Boulton, for being so solid. For Ron and Rod. For David, Steve, Henry and Alan, the thoroughbred. For all of them. They were all brilliant. They gave me so much.

The press were knocking around the party just in case what happened happened and I was snapped cuddling Des Anderson, cuddling Bruce, cuddling Franny, cuddling the waitress, cuddling a bottle. I am told I was dancing on the floor to the Bay City Rollers. That's how drunk I had become.

CHAPTER FOURTEEN

The Sack

Feeling great pride at being manager of the English champions, I took a relaxing holiday up in Edinburgh during the summer. My mind was very much on the coming season. Roy McFarland was back from injury. I was feeling very confident. We were in the European Cup and I very much wanted to win it. I thought we could. Matt Busby's Manchester United and Jock Stein's Celtic were still the only two British clubs to bring it back to these islands. We were playing wonderful football in the second half of our Championship campaign, certainly as good as anything on the Continent, but I did feel that an addition or two to the squad might now be appropriate for the challenge ahead.

I had an idea of the sort of player I was looking for. Earlier, I had tried to sign Peter Osgood. I knew him well from old Spurs and Chelsea ding-dongs and admired him, for he was a big, strong man, but had the deft touch and skills of a slightly built Continental player. He scored some magical goals and could turn a game. I always felt that the harder the opponents, the better he would play. England wasted him as a resource. Ossie had a reputation as a lively character on and off the field, but all that rubbish never bothered me. We met at the Hyde Park Hotel in London when Peter was particularly unsettled at Chelsea, but he eventually decided to join Lawrie McMenemy at Southampton.

Sitting up in Scotland, I was leafing through the newspapers when I spotted a small snippet that said that Charlie George was on the point of leaving Arsenal for £100,000. Charlie was another one I hugely admired and very much in the same mould as Osgood. Full of flair and fun, he was a tall, galloping centre-forward who scored spectacular goals and could change the course of a game. His work rate was phenomenal. Even though he was a key player in Arsenal's Double-winning side, he too had been ignored by the England managers. Perhaps Alf Ramsey and Don Revie disapproved of his long hair or his habit of speaking his mind.

I rang Des Anderson. 'The papers are saying that Charlie George is about to sign for someone for £100,000. That's a snip. See if you can get hold of him.'

Des agreed and managed to contact Charlie. When he called back, I could tell by his voice that the news was not good.

'He's agreed terms with Terry Neill.'

Terry Neill was manager of Spurs. That was enough for me. I jumped in the car and sped down to London. Charlie was a mad Gooner. He loved Arsenal and I knew he would not be leaving Highbury happily. I also knew that, as a product of the North Bank, Tottenham Hotspur would not be his first choice of club. The man was not thinking straight.

Hours later, when I got in front of Charlie, he was pleased to see me and I immediately tried to sell him Derby County. Not the club – the vision. It was not hard: we were champions after all and in Europe.

'Dave, I wish you'd come in earlier. I'd love to play for you and for Derby. Really. But I've agreed terms with Terry Neill.'

'Yes, but have you signed?'

'Not exactly. I would have signed yesterday when we agreed terms, but Terry wanted me to come back tomorrow when he could arrange for the press to be around.'

I pulled a pen from my breast pocket and a hastily prepared draft contract with lots of blank spaces from my inside pocket and passed it to Charlie. He smiled at me and then signed. Moral of the story for managers: if you have the player you want, never put off the physical signing. Not even for one day.

Charlie scored on his League debut in the first match of the season away to Sheffield United and, as I fully expected, the Derby crowd immediately fell in love with him. He finished that season as Derby's top scorer and my enduring image of Charlie is him holding his arms aloft and grinning widely after he had scored, with his now permed locks bouncing down on his shoulders. Charlie had a perm that rivalled Kevin Keegan's. It was all very *Starsky and Hutch*. Very 1970s. Even Henry Cooper would have sported a perm if nature had permitted it.

Charlie may have had his best ever game in the October of 1975. I certainly consider it the best game I presided over as a manager. In round one of the European Cup, we lost by a single goal to Slovan Bratislava at their place but managed to overcome them by three goals to nil at the Baseball Ground. The scene was set for the first leg of the second round at the Baseball Ground, where we would entertain Real Madrid.

Real had dominated European football for decades and boasted among their team Gunter Netzer, Paul Breitner, Miguel Angel and Pirri. We were not expected to beat them. That night, 35,000 crammed into the Baseball Ground and had to wait only 10 minutes for Charlie to crack a left-foot volley past Angel. It was a searing strike. Before they could recover their composure, Franny Lee was tripped in the penalty area and Charlie, as cool as a cucumber, made it 2–0. Pirri then pulled a goal back for Madrid, but just before half-time David Nish gave us a third. In the dressing-room at half-time, the adrenalin was coursing through our veins. We were electrifying, but Madrid were not lying back and taking it. They were more than capable of getting back into the game and claiming it. They nearly did when Pirri had a goal disallowed that looked all right to me, but we knocked the match on the head when Kevin Hector was brought down in the penalty area. Charlie stepped forward and put it away surely. I don't think

Charlie George scored many hat-tricks in his career, but trust him to get one against Real Madrid. They all played a blinder that evening. Nishy and Colin Todd were masterful in defence. Colin Boulton was world-class in goal. They couldn't make Archie Gemmill out. You see him here. You see him there. And Kevin up front. Kevin was an ordinary bloke. He could have got a job as a full-time police identity parade member. He did not stand out in a crowd, but he was no ordinary footballer. I class him up there with Jimmy Greaves among the all-time greatest natural goalscorers I have ever seen.

It was 4–1. We had left them with a mountain to climb back at the Bernabéu. We should have remembered, though, that we were playing the footballing equivalent of Sir Edmund Hillary because they climbed that mountain by thrashing us 5–1 and putting us out of the European Cup 6–5 on aggregate. In our defence, we had lost Bruce Rioch and Franny Lee through injury, and I refused to instruct the team to play defensively or adopt any time-wasting tactics. I got some stick over this. These days, it would be very rare for a team to surrender a three-goal lead. But my whole football breeding was always to entertain, to play fairly and to give one's all. Never did Tommy Walker, Bill Nicholson or Brian Clough tell us to waste time or adopt cynical defensive tactics. When I see the best teams in the country doing it nowadays, it makes me seethe.

Domestically, we were still going great guns and were up there with the leaders Liverpool, Queens Park Rangers and Manchester United. We put together a good FA Cup run in the new year and the Double was still very much on the cards, right up until April, four weeks before the end of the season. Having disposed of Everton, Liverpool, Southend and Newcastle in the FA Cup, we finally fell to my old pal Tommy Docherty's remodelled Manchester United side in the semi-final. This was the year that United themselves were beaten by Second Division underdogs Southampton (featuring Peter Osgood) in the final.

Around this time, we played Leeds United in an extremely physical game. We were used to matches against Leeds being like this, but that day they were particularly unpleasant. I watched as

Norman Hunter, United's underfed Doberman, snapped away at Franny Lee. I was not surprised when one tussle blew up and Franny was left with a split lip. I was watching from the stand that afternoon and tried to get down to the pitch, but I was not fast enough. Franny had retaliated and both players were sent off. Back in the dressing-room, I had never seen him so incensed. The walls of the changing-rooms were thin at the Baseball Ground and I was seriously concerned that he was going to bash his way through them to get at Hunter. I had to leave Roy McFarland guarding him. After the match had finished, Franny had calmed down, but was determined to fight Norman outside, 'man to man' and 'on the cobbles'. I was tempted to arrange it.

Losing to Manchester United in the FA Cup semi-final seemed to shatter our confidence and we lost three of our five remaining League games. Although we won with a flourish 6–2 at Ipswich on the last day, we were out of the title race and ended up in fourth position. Of course, I was disappointed that we had come out of the season with no trophies. We all were. But I did not regard it as a failure and certainly we had all enjoyed ourselves and acquitted ourselves well. We had done well in the League and the FA Cup, and had had a memorable European Cup run. Sadly, failure is relative and there were some people on the board at Derby County who believed it was necessary to win something every year. In that scorching close season when the rivers dried up, houses started subsiding and the police patrolled residential streets looking for house-owners sneakily watering their gardens, I started to hear the whispers again. Bring Back Clough.

My position was not helped by our subdued start to the 1976–77 season. We drew the first three matches, lost the next two and then drew two more. We didn't record our first victory of the campaign until October. That was against Tottenham and we absolutely caned them 8–2. The only surviving player from my time was big Pat Jennings in goal. I really felt for him. I'm sure he had rarely conceded as many goals in his entire career. Whilst I was delighted that Bruce Rioch hammered home four, Charlie George two and Colin Todd and Rod Thomas one each, I really wanted them to stop. Nobody likes to see a friend in discomfort.

A wee man on the pitch bustling away against the odds up-front aroused my sympathy. For this was Alfie Conn Jnr, son of my old teammate and Hearts legend Alfie Conn Snr. Fortunately for me, Bill Nicholson was no longer at the helm because if he had been I would have felt very, very uncomfortable. If I thought I had difficulties, this was nothing to what Spurs were facing. The end of the season would see them rock-bottom of the First Division and relegated for the first time in a quarter of a century. It was a depressing time for all those connected with the club. Fortunately, they were able to build a new team around the one man that did stand out like a beacon with his incredible passing in that 8–2 defeat – Glenn Hoddle – and bounce straight back. Once they added their two Argentinian imports, Ardiles and Villa, they were soon back on top of their game.

Despite the convincing win over Spurs, we were in the lower half of the Division and this supplied welcome ammunition for some people in the club who wanted me out. I don't think they had anything against me personally. I was merely a barrier to their dream of Brian Clough returning being realised. Brian had left Brighton and taken over at Leeds United for a famous but short period. He had taken John McGovern and John O'Hare with him, but still found resistance from the players who had not forgotten that Brian had spent some seasons, not so long ago, attacking their style of play and the Don Revie regime in general. Legend has it that, when he first arrived and addressed the players, he told them they could throw their medals in the bin, as they had been won dishonestly. This was not the best start to their relationship. Team and manager divorced before the marriage could be consummated. Brian was now almost next door to Derby at Nottingham Forest and he was already making them look good. Some people at Derby believed Brian was just waiting to return to his spiritual football home and now was the time to push me out and welcome him back in before he and Forest became too attached or, God forbid, Forest and Derby passed each other going in opposite directions up and down the Football League motorway.

I was aware of this and also aware that these sentiments had only been silenced because it was impossible to argue with the club's achievements since Brian left. What did make me angry and upset was that the knives were out at the first run of bad form. We were not seriously threatened with relegation. We traditionally played better after Christmas than before and we still had a squad which was the envy of most clubs. I heard whispered criticisms of Des and myself. I was getting stick for paying £300,000 for Leighton James of Burnley. Leighton was a fast Welsh winger who had shone every time I had seen him play and had impressed the country with some virtuoso performances for his club and country that were televised. At Derby, as yet, he had not quite lived up to his promise. Remarks had also been made about my weight. I was now in middle-age and no longer playing. These things happen. Someone told me the board were concerned that I went out too much! Went out too much? I was in my 40s, not an impressionable apprentice. It was all petty stuff, but the wind was changing and it was getting stronger.

One day, in November 1976, I was sitting in my office at the Baseball Ground. I was a bit down. Although our League performances were picking up, AEK Athens had just dumped us out of the UEFA Cup. I was preparing for our regular board meeting, where all the club issues of the week would be discussed. Frank Cholorton walked in and dropped a folded up copy of *The Sun* on my desk. Frank was a great friend of mine and a great friend of Derby County. He pointed to a small paragraph, entitled 'Beware of the Bogeyman', written by John Sadler. It basically said that a contact of his had been playing golf with some directors of an East Midlands club and they had revealed that their team manager would be receiving his cards imminently. Poor Frank, he was not stirring the pot, he was being a friend and, just in case there was any truth in the report, he did not want me walking into the lion's den totally unprepared.

The report was obviously about Derby and me. My directors had been playing golf the previous day. Anger descended and I felt my heart thumping against my chest wall. The buggers could sack me, but telling *The Sun* before they told me was unforgivable. But typical. I burst into the boardroom with the newspaper rolled up in my fist. I was not sure where I was going to put it.

'This John Sadler thing,' I shouted. 'This is you lot, isn't it.' I was telling, not asking. The embarrassed shuffling of bottoms on seats and the sudden need to screw tops back onto pens said it all.

'You can stick your job up your arse.'

I turned around, went back to my office and sat back in my chair, trembling. Never before had I experienced such an urge to break human jaws. Frank Cholorton was still lingering around, scared to say a word, but with the look of a man who was asking himself just what he had triggered.

As my first rush of temper subsided, common sense and pragmatism entered the equation for the first time. I had just jacked in my job. I had a wife, a family, a mortgage and a dog. By implication, I had committed not just myself but Des Anderson to the dole queue. By resigning, I had forfeited any financial settlement. I jumped back up and burst into the boardroom again. This time the directors looked around for any exit that I was not blocking. 'I don't resign. You have to sack me.'

Sam Longson came back with me into the office and tried to pacify me and get me back on side. But he and I both knew the game was up. He was no longer as powerful at Derby as he once was.

'Good day?' smiled Isobel when I returned home from work. She had been busy supervising the work we were having done on a dream home we were having built in Derby. 'Not great,' I replied as I sunk into the armchair.

Sadly, there was no threatened strike from the players, although Charlie George in particular made his unhappiness about the situation public. There was certainly no Bring Back Mackay campaign. I began to feel very unwanted. Christmas in 1976 was a strange one. It was my first Christmas without being in work ever. Whilst it was a relief to have a break from the pressures of football management, this was the first time I had not been involved in the game since I was a boy and, more importantly, the first time I had been out of work. It was a frightening and salutary experience. I had thought that job offers would be piling up on my doormat and the phone would be red hot. Our postman must have wondered what was happening each morning when he stuffed our bills through the letter box and this figure through the frosted glass on the other side of the door pulled them from his hand before he could let go. I suppose I was bitter. We had to abandon the building of the house and this was only slightly less expensive than finishing it. Having no income quickly saps any confidence you have about the future. I took some small comfort from the fact that the Derby directors did not get their own way completely. Brian Clough did not leave Forest to rejoin Derby County. He stayed to finish what he started at Nottingham and within a few years would take them to even greater heights than he had Derby. The club would become champions of Europe whilst Derby County would sadly slide down as far as the Third Division.

Ken Wheldon had made his money in haulage and, like many self-made men of the time, he drove an obligatory Rolls-Royce and owned his local football team. His club was Walsall, then struggling against relegation in the Third Division. When Ken pulled his Roller up outside my house in March 1977, I was keen to hear what he had to say following his introductory telephone call. A couple of people had told me that Ken was so tight that on rainy days he switched off his windscreen wipers when he passed under railway tunnels. The offer he made me was not at all parsimonious. There were eight games left until the end of the season and he offered me a mouth-watering sum if I could save the club from relegation. I had no fear of a payment-by-results arrangement whatsoever. I had no choice either. My £5,000 pay-off from Derby was running out fast and that very special phone call from the White Hart Lane area of north London that I had secretly been hoping for had not materialised. I accepted Ken's offer. I asked Isobel to put the spam away and cook some steak instead for a change.

After four games, Walsall had got enough points to put them into safety and Ken was as good as his word and paid me my bonus. We ended up finishing well clear of the drop at 15th. Walsall were a homely club nestled in the Black Country in their then Fellows Park ground. They had never played in the First Division and never won the FA Cup, so, unlike Forest or Derby, there was no pressure to bring back the good times. There had been none in particular. When Ken asked me to sign up for the following season, I was excited to do so. We had some good players, especially the young striker Alan Buckley, and I persuaded my old colleague Jimmy Robertson from Spurs to join us before hanging up his boots altogether. I also picked up Jeff King, Henry Newton and Tony Macken from Derby, where Tommy Docherty was now in charge and buying and selling players like there was no tomorrow.

The 1977–78 season turned out better than I could have imagined. We played well all season and were in touch with the race for promotion, which was a real improvement on the previous term. We ended up finishing sixth. However, the highlight of the season was a memorable run in the FA Cup, where we finally lost out to the eventual finalists Arsenal at Highbury after putting out Leicester City, another First Division side. For a Third Division side to make the fifth round of the FA Cup was quite an achievement and, remember, as a Third Division club we had to compete from the first round not the third.

I remember the Arsenal game well. There was quite a lot of publicity before the match because Walsall had knocked the Gunners out of the FA Cup some 40 years earlier in one of the most famous acts of giant-killing ever. Herbert Chapman's side, with the likes of Eddie Hapgood, George Male, Alex James and Cliff Bastin, were considered invincible, but little Walsall managed to win. No such luck this time around. Arsenal could boast Pat Jennings in goal (now enjoying what would be a long Indian summer at Highbury after finally leaving Spurs), David O'Leary, Liam Brady, Frank Stapleton and Malcolm Macdonald. Any side that could afford to have Alan Hudson sitting on the bench were not short of talent. They tore us apart and were 3–0 up at half-time. If it hadn't been for the superb efforts of Mick Kearns in goal, it might have been ten. Alan Buckley pulled one back for us just after half-time and we did well to stop Arsenal scoring any more than the one more they finally got. Our defender

Colin Harrison had a great game for us, as did two old First Division veterans Mick Bates, formerly of Leeds United, and Alun Evans, once of Liverpool.

We were all happy with the progress made at Walsall and I was looking forward to the 1978–79 season. I thought we had a realistic chance of getting out of the Third Division and was happy to rebuild my managerial career over at Fellows Park. Then came another one of those phone calls that changes the course of your life. It was an Arab gentleman called Mousa Raschid and he asked me to meet him and his friend at a London hotel. He said it was about a 'footballing matter'. I took Des with me just in case it was an elaborate kidnap plot (although I couldn't imagine who would pay the ransom) and we sat in the lounge area of the Park Lane Hilton full of anticipation. Mr Raschid arrived with a distinguished-looking man whom he introduced as Mohammed Al-Mulla. Mr Al-Mulla was the chairman of Al-Arabi, one of the big two football clubs in Kuwait.

'It is the greatest honour to meet you. You are a hero,' smiled Mohammed. I looked over my shoulder to see if he was addressing someone sitting behind me. It emerged that Mohammed had been educated in London during the early 1960s and had visited White Hart Lane and fallen in love with the Double-winning Spurs side. He knew his onions. He had taken his love of football back to Kuwait and had been instrumental in developing the game in his home country.

'We would like to offer you the job of manager of Al-Arabi – are you interested?' I soon learnt that Arabs in general, whilst highly polite, do not beat about the bush. I replied that it would depend.

'How much do you want?' he said.

'Forty thousand,' I returned immediately. Des almost choked on his coffee.

'That's fine,' replied Mousa Raschid almost as quickly. I wrote the figure down on a napkin just to make sure there was no confusion.

'Oh, £40,000,' said Mousa, 'I thought you said £14,000. We shall have to give that some consideration. Thank you. We will respond to you shortly.'

After much handshaking and goodbyes, Des and I sat back down.

'You blew it there,' Des sighed. In 1978, £40,000 was a huge amount of money. It would buy you a nice detached house even in the south of England. It was certainly more than I had ever earned in salary and it would be tax-free.

'If they really want us, Des, they'll pay it.'

'Us?'

'Well, you're coming, aren't you?'

I was totally open with Ken Wheldon about the approach that had been made and he said that, if they really came through with an offer of that magnitude, it was the chance of a lifetime and he would advise me to take it. Always a shrewd businessman, he urged me to insist on a quarter of the first year's money up front. I hadn't thought of that but, as he said, I had no recourse to English contract law should they get rid of me after five games. I did not want to leave Walsall, but the Derby experience had hardened me up to the facts of life as a manager, and about the security of employment and opportunities for earning regular wages in professional football.

Sure enough, two weeks later Mousa Raschid rang and said that they agreed to my terms and had even acceded the up-front cash payment. I asked for £12,000, anticipating they would knock me down to £10,000, but they didn't. I had never seen so much cash and found myself heading towards Knightsbridge and Harrods to spend it. Isobel managed to drag me out before I could do too much damage. By now, Des had a pub in Derby and had decided not to accompany me, but Neil Martin, who was a good friend and had played under me at Forest, was keen to move into the management game and came along. So we set off alone to start a new life on the other side of the world. Our families would be joining us just as soon as we had settled in. As the plane gathered height at take-off, I can remember thinking: 'What have you done now, Mackay?'

CHAPTER FIFTEEN

Gulf not Golf

The contrast between Walsall and Kuwait could not have been greater: the sun shone in Kuwait, for one. The buildings were tall and new. The cars long and sleek. It was a different world altogether. Everyone wore flowing thobes and headgear – the men in light colours and the women in dark ones. There was therefore no concern over who was wearing the best designer clothes. There was no real competition either over physical looks for the women, as most of them wore yashmaks covering their whole face bar their eyes. The place exuded serious wealth wherever you looked. Kuwait was oil rich and it seemed like its population could not spend its money fast enough. Luxury hotels and state-of-the-art glass corporate skyscrapers stood side by side. Expatriates and locals alike popped into the Hilton for coffee as casually as people at home pick up a snack from their local Greggs. I adapted to the new culture very quickly. I learnt that there was no need to rush. That people liked to stop and talk. I quickly understood about religious festivals, such as Ramadan and Eid, and what a large part religion plays generally in the everyday lives of the Muslim people. The wailing call of the mosque at worship time became as familiar to me as the sound of church bells at home. We soon made many friends among the Kuwaiti people and we would spend eight very happy years there. From the first day, they showed us great respect and friendship, and made us feel completely welcome in their country. The cultural tensions between the East and West that have become such a worry as I write never seemed to encroach upon us in Kuwait at that time. We never ever feared for our personal safety. The English (the concept of a Scotsman was not really recognised) were almost revered and were certainly top of the pecking order of respect among the expatriates. A lovely man called Brian Doyle was already in the country coaching and he and his family became our close friends and helped us settle in rapidly.

I did learn straight away that Arabs, whilst not intending to be rude, spoke as they saw. When I was being shown around the Al-Arabi ground for the first time, I was introduced to one of the club officials. He looked me up and down. 'You very fat,' he announced.

'I'm the coach, not a player,' I replied defensively.

But he was right, I was very fat. But not for long. Without trying, the pounds literally fell away as I changed my diet to less fatty foods, no alcohol and generally, with the hot climate, only really ate once a day. By the time Isobel and the kids arrived, they could not believe the change in me.

'Dad, where did your body go?' asked young Julie, innocently.

All the players were local lads and played part-time. Most were at the university or training to be engineers, architects, accountants or bankers. Others were soldiers and policemen. There were some good players among them and I was pleasantly surprised at the standard they had reached. The three big clubs in the country were Al-Qadissiya, Kuwait City and ourselves, and when they met, crowds of up to 20,000 would pack into the grounds for the match. When I took over, Al-Arabi had finished mid-table in the Kuwaiti league and the objective of my appointment was to build a club that could challenge Kuwait City and the other big rival Al-Qadissiya for the title and overall dominance of football in the country. My assistant was Ali Mullar and he proved to be an invaluable help to me in communicating with the players, especially in the early days. At the end of the 1978–79 season, my first in the Middle East, we needed to beat Kuwait City in the last match of the season to win the Championship, but only managed a draw. Still, we were runners-up and the next season we did it. In over eight years with Al-Arabi, we won the Treble, the Championship five times in all, the first-ever Gulf Cup, the Emiri Cup and some other competitions.

The supporters and all the patrons of the club were eternally grateful. One of our patrons was Sheikh Fahd, who was a member of the Royal family, and he invited me to take tea with the Emir at the peak of our success. The Emir was the ruler, and taking tea with him and chatting football was the equivalent of sitting in Buckingham Palace with the Queen. Sheikh Fahd was a lovely man who had a passion for football, and it was with utter horror that we were informed many years later, that when Iraq finally invaded Kuwait, the first thing that Saddam Hussein's son Uday did was travel to Sheikh Fahd's palace and shoot him personally. Uday had taken a dislike to Sheikh Fahd when the Kuwaiti national team had beaten his Iraqi football team in a so-called friendly match.

At one point, Geoff Hurst, formerly of West Ham and renowned for his World Cup hat-trick, came out to manage Kuwait City, along with his assistant John Cartwright. I had dinner with him and his wife Judith. They were considering the terms that they had been offered.

'It's good money,' said Geoff, 'but I'm not sure it is enough to uproot and cut our ties at home.'

'Then ask for more. If they really want you, they will pay it,' I advised. Geoff hadn't yet got his head around the Arab custom of bargaining. 'Nobody's first price is their last. They expect you to bargain. They enjoy it.' Geoff got his improved terms.

I parted company with Al-Arabi very amicably in 1986, when Shabab Club of Dubai persuaded me to come to the United Arab Emirates and manage them. My eight years in Kuwait had been extremely successful and prosperous, but I was now 52 years old and I wanted a new challenge and new experiences. It seemed an age since I had worked in England. Eight years really is a long time in football and Kuwait really is a long way from home. Although I kept in touch with what was happening at home, nobody there really knew or cared what was happening in the Middle East. I was a forgotten man as far as British football was concerned. I never worked in Saudi Arabia, but I have lost count of the amount of times people have asked me how I enjoyed living in Saudi – it being the only Middle Eastern country that the average Brit at home could name with confidence. Events later in the 1990s and the Gulf War obviously changed all that.

Neil Martin went with me to Shabab and we were soon joined by Joe Kinnear, my old Spurs mate, who coached the kids. Shabab's team was not as good or as developed as Al-Arabi and I had a bigger task turning them around. When I had not achieved results by the end of the first season, they sacked me. They had every right, too, as they were paying serious money for my services and I had no complaint. At that time in my life, I was perfectly content to ride with my destiny.

We came back to England with mixed feelings. Nearly a decade away had made us hardened expatriates. We were used to viewing events in Britain from a safe distance and had a BBC World Service perspective on our home country. We were used to beaches, sun, dinner parties, empty roads, barbecues and American TV programmes. We'd missed the whole Thatcher revolution up to then. We looked forward to seeing a real-life yuppie, clutching a Filofax. In football, Brian Clough had turned Nottingham Forest into European champions and he still grabbed most of the headlines. Liverpool grabbed most of the trophies. Hooligans ran amok. Fortunately, I had had a decade of earning good money and therefore was not returning home with an urgent financial need to work, but I still considered myself a young man (still do) and wanted to work again. I was surprised at how quickly I received the first offer. Doncaster Rovers were a well-supported club in the Fourth Division and they invited Joe Kinnear and me to join them. As usual, they had no money and were finding it difficult to survive. One of the first things the board wanted me to do was to sell players to raise funds. I told them I could get £30,000 for a lad called Brian Deane and they laughed at me. Sheffield United took him and he became the scorer of the first-ever Premiership goal. When he moved on from Bramall Lane, it was for more than £1 million. In my short stay with Rovers, I also sold Rufus Brevett. It seems ironic to talk about the good players I sold for Doncaster Rovers, but when the choice is selling your best players or having no club, the former is far more attractive.

At this point, Ken Wheldon came into my life again. He was always delighted with what I had done for him at Walsall and now he was on the board at Birmingham City, where he had brought in the Kumar brothers and in turn they had brought in their money. The Blues were a big club with serious committed support, although they did not share the same illustrious history as neighbours Aston Villa and West Bromwich Albion. The problem was they had fallen into the Third Division for the first time in their history and morale was at an all-time low. He asked me to take over and I did – leaving Joe at the helm at Doncaster.

Again, I believed that Birmingham could be revived. All big clubs can. Good crowds can help sides win – that is a fact and I have known mediocre teams win time and time again as their supporters literally willed them to do so. Teams that do well, but do not have a core committed support, never last too long at the top. The fans at St Andrews are among the most passionate in the country and, when I got there, their passion had fermented into anger. They were in the wrong place and knew it, and demanded an immediate return to the top echelons. Although I knew I would have to work fast, I relished the challenge. Bobby Ferguson, the former Derby player and Ipswich manager, joined me as my deputy. In my two seasons at the club, sadly I could not deliver automatic promotion and we finished seventh and then twelfth. As far as most people were concerned, that was going backwards and I jumped just as I was being pushed. I was a bit peeved because we'd just completed a twelve-match unbeaten run. The fact that eight of those twelve matches were draws didn't help, though. I'm not sure in which way this might be significant, but in the season after I left, the Blues were finally promoted back into the new First Division.

Luckily for me, an Egyptian club called Zamalek had offered me a job. Back in England, my stints with Doncaster and Birmingham had been far from distinguished, but in the Middle East I was still hot property. Every other Middle Eastern club with any aspirations wanted to emulate what Al-Arabi had done and I was the man that had made it happen in their eyes. Egypt was a very different country to Kuwait. Comparing Kuwait City with Cairo is like comparing Milton Keynes with deepest Bermondsey. There were millions more cars on the congested Cairo roads and many of the models were straight out of the 1950s. They zig-zagged around the streets, competing with children, chickens, donkeys, goats and horse-and-carriage cabbies for road space. Unlike Kuwait's air of wealth and modernity, Cairo exuded a happy poverty. I was surprised to find that some people knew who I was and we fell in love with the place straight away.

The reason some people in Egypt knew me was because in November 1962, nearly 30 years earlier, Tottenham Hotspur had played Zamalek in a friendly. We won 7–3 in a game that I can barely recall, but Jimmy Greaves scored twice, as did Terry Dyson, and John White netted one of the others. I soon learnt that this was Zamelek's finest moment and that the game was regularly replayed on Egyptian television and referred to in the media. Yellowed and fading newspaper cuttings of the game could still be seen stuck to walls, edges curling, in barber shops and cafés. The players in that Zamalek team were national heroes. I didn't like to tell anyone it was a friendly and, being in the middle of a League season when we were defending our Double-winning status, we probably weren't trying very hard. That wouldn't have been very nice.

Zamalek's archenemies were Al-Ahli and the relationship between these two Cairo clubs was not dissimilar to that of Celtic and Rangers. The fans were maniacal in their hatred for one another and it was not safe around the streets adjoining either stadium when these two clubs met. I realised I had entered new footballing territory when one of my Egyptian colleagues, referring to a game before my time, by way of explanation said to another colleague: 'You remember, the game when the referee was shot.'

I breathed a sigh of relief when we beat Al-Ahli in our first meeting under my tenure. My opposite number at Al-Ahli, Mike Everett, was not so lucky. He was promptly fired. Allan Harris, brother of Chelsea's Ronnie 'Chopper' Harris, came in to replace him.

We lived in a plush apartment in a tower block some floors up. One afternoon, I was having a nap when I awoke to some loud rumbling noises. The air-conditioning system was pretty primitive and prone to gurgling, but Isobel burst into the room with my daughter Julie who was out on holiday with her family.

'David, I don't like this. Get up, I think we're having an earthquake.'

'Don't be silly, woman. It's the air-con.' I turned over and attempted to go back to sleep.

A few minutes later, I felt the bed move. I jumped up and there was no sign of Isobel or the kids. I looked out of the window and could see them down below waving up at me, so I waved back. I realised they were screaming at me, so I went downstairs where they explained that our building, which was 16 storeys high, had leant over and touched the building next to it. That was my first earthquake.

Success came fast at Zamalek. My assistant was a famous Egyptian footballer by the name of Farouk Gaffer. The Egyptians called him 'The Prince' and he was a national hero. We made a good partnership. The Egyptian game was more mature and therefore more developed than in Kuwait or the United Arab Emirates. There were some exceptional young footballers around and I managed to motivate and develop a strong team very quickly. In the two years I was around, we won the Egyptian League twice. I couldn't really do much more. But it was not enough. We had our big game against Al-Ahli in my final season and within the first few minutes our centre-back got himself sent off. At half-time, I thought to be trailing only 1–0 was not bad, seeing it was ten men against eleven. We crumbled a bit towards the end of the match and lost 3–0. I knew there would be trouble but thought that the directors would see this one defeat in the perspective of what had been achieved at the club over the last two years. The directors asked to see me after the game. I told them that I would see them in the morning. I'm sure that did not help. The following morning, I faced them. I had hoped that they may have slept on the defeat and were seeing it in a more reflective light.

'We'd like to know why we lost yesterday.'

'Simple. They had eleven men. We had ten.'

'This is not a good enough reason.'

I was not about to grovel. I shrugged my shoulders. Maybe that gesture has some rude significance in Egypt that had passed me by. It was at that point they got angry and I lost my job. It was Allan Harris's turn to feel bad.

It was a great shame that my time at Zamalek ended with a silly little bit of unpleasantness because I had a very happy time at the club and we were good for each other. I am told by friends who have visited Egypt for holidays that matches from my reign have finally replaced the Spurs friendly in the affections of Zamalek fans and that I am still held in high esteem by many. That is nice to know.

Next up was Qatar. They approached me to coach their youth international side on a short-term contract and I spent my last year in management with them. Qatar is a small Middle Eastern country, wealthy and keen to modernise. It was like a smaller version of Kuwait. They wanted to develop their game in line with their neighbours. Other old chums from the English game managing clubs out there were Graham Williams and Len Ashurst, good defenders at West Bromwich Albion and Sunderland respectively in the 1960s. George Blues, a Scot, came out as my assistant, and he and his family became great friends. George went on to become a successful coach at the Indian side FC Kochin. We did a good job with the youngsters and guided them to World Cup qualification for the first time. A lad called Rene Meulensteen joined us, coaching the young kids, and he had a real flair for it. Years later, I recommended him to Sir Alex

Ferguson and he works with Alex to this day.

While I was there, I developed a cold sore on my lip that refused to heal. The hospital in Qatar did a fair job stitching the lip up and in the summer of 1996 my contract was up and we returned home unsure of what would happen next. I was now 62 years old, but still fit, alert and in possession of all my marbles. I was not really ready for growing marrows or whatever it is retired people are expected to do. Events overtook me. First, Al-Arabi contacted me and offered me my old job back. It was a great feeling and, although my natural instinct is not to return to somewhere I have had great success – because it will always be almost impossible to emulate it – I was very tempted. Then my lip flared up again and Isobel insisted I attend the City Hospital in Nottingham before we made any decision.

They performed a biopsy, which was enough in itself to send a shiver down my spine. Notwithstanding broken legs and babies being born, I had barely seen the inside of a hospital. Although I was in my 60s, on the inside I remained a teenager and therefore did not expect to experience health problems. When they told me I had cancer and that I would have to be treated with a course of radiation, I was knocked for six. Not in a feeling-sorry-for-myself sort of way, but in a what-a-bloody-nuisance sort of a way. They asked me if I smoked a pipe (apparently this form of cancer was common in pipe-smokers). I never have. Isobel puts it down to the sun and the time I went to South Africa in the 1950s and came back with burnt lips. I'm not so sure. If that is the case, then it sure had a long incubation period. The doctors advised that it would be prudent to keep away from the sun and therefore helped make our minds up about the Kuwaiti offer.

Thankfully, I completed the course of radiation and it seemed to do the trick. During my treatment, I was shocked to find that there were so many forms of cancer. I had assumed it was mainly restricted to internal organs, but I found out that if you've got it – you can get cancer of it. Ears, noses, eyes, mouth – I won't go on.

I am forever in the debt of Mr Chan, who was my wonderful oncologist, and the teams of radiologists and nurses that looked after me and all the other patients. These people, and there are thousands of them in hospitals up and down Britain, really are the unsung heroes of our country. They don't score goals or make pop records, but their contribution to our society dwarfs anything in the entertainment industry. They are there for all of us when we need them. Someone else was there for me too – Isobel. Without her love, care and absolute faith in my full recovery, I'm sure I would have struggled both mentally and physically. I called her Doctor Mackay because I appreciated the potency of her course of treatment. Never underestimate the love of a good woman.

Professionally, it was the end of the road, although I was offered a job in Oman. By then, however, the situation in the Middle East was worsening and, although Oman has always been relatively peaceful, we decided that the region was too volatile at that time. I had a few problems adjusting to relative inactivity, but I had had a good run and there was much to be thankful for. Football, the game I loved and continue to love, had given me a living for nearly half a century. I'd achieved many things and made my mark. What more can a man ask? I have a wonderful family and we have all enjoyed good times and good health. We have grandchildren now to keep us occupied. I lost my mum and dad along the way, as did Isobel, but few people in their 60s still have parents around. That's being greedy. But it doesn't stop you missing them and not a day goes by when we don't think about all four of them. Mum went first and I was devastated because I did not expect it. I still miss her now. I was lucky enough to have quality time with Dad after she died and I was able to take him to the Middle East, where he spent long spells with me. Isobel, too, had lost her parents by then.

But I have my health. I go for a run every day. I travel back and forth from Nottingham to Edinburgh. Sometimes I go down to London. I attend Derby home games, although at the time of writing I'm not sure that it is good for my health. I like attending reunions and functions because I get to see my old pals. Old being the appropriate word. One of the disturbing things about being my age is that more of my friends are dead than alive. The dead ones are the more difficult to contact.

I still love the game of football even though it has changed almost beyond recognition from my day. The only roasting we

ever did was the occasional chestnut at Christmas and the only
snorting I recall was bent over a bowl of Friar's Balsam with a
towel over my head when trying to throw off a bad cold.
Premiership footballers earn more in a week now than Tottenham
paid Hearts for me in 1959 and that was a record for a defender
back then. The sort of money getting paid to footballers is
ridiculous and it is no wonder they lose sight of the real world and
the rules, regulations and codes most of us choose to live by.
Imagine a group of young bricklayers, carpenters and labourers
working on building an extension on your house. Imagine you
started to pay them £30,000 a week instead of the £500 they
thought they would get. What would happen? They'd go berserk.
They would not be able to cope. As quickly as they could spend
money, they'd accumulate it to a level they could not ever
visualise and all in an incredibly short space of time. They'd begin
to think they were special; that they could do what they want.
Young people are reckless by nature and to bestow such riches on
them is irresponsible of us as a society. Remember that these
footballers would have been those bricklayers, carpenters and
labourers if it wasn't for the fact they could kick a ball better than
their peers.

I remember when *Match of the Day* started and the party-
poopers complained that television would kill the game as a
spectator sport. I disagreed then, but can see the case now. *Match
of the Day* was great because it allowed people that could not get
to games to see their teams and heroes in action. It made stars and
household names of hundreds and it recorded for posterity the
great moments. Televised football was a definite boost for the
game, but it was restricted mainly to highlights and only a couple
of games a week at that. It was the perfect taster. Now every game
of significance (and plenty that are not) is broadcast live and in its
entirety. Never again will anyone miss a goal because they went
for a pee. Never again will anyone not be sure whether a ball went
over the line or not. We pump it out, almost choke on it and then
dissect it to death. No wonder you cannot help but see the huge
swathes of empty seats that stand out like sores at nearly all
grounds when the cameras are present. They make me wince.

Why pay the money to go when you can watch it all from your armchair? With all this money going out to the players seemingly being financed by the television companies rather than the spectators coming through the turnstiles, what happens when viewing figures recede and the TV companies do not want to pay as much? Hasn't this started already?

In Scotland, gates are very low and sliding, and I find this particularly sad. Football bound our communities together and gave us pride and purpose. Now, every other club depends on the visits of Celtic and Rangers to balance their books. This is why we have engineered a fixture system that allows the clubs to have several pops at the big two. The gulf between Celtic and Rangers and the rest in terms of quality, finance and support is now more polarised than at any other time. As I write, it seems hard to imagine a time when Rangers could catch up with Celtic even. Whilst I relish great football sides, I believe it is unhealthy for the game to have such immovable differences in class in the top echelons. It kills the allure of the game. Local boys know that the chances of breaking into the team at Celtic or Rangers are virtually non-existent, but are they going to get sufficiently excited about the prospect of playing for Motherwell, for example, to devote their lives to playing football? Is there a boy today, lying in bed dreaming of pulling on a Hearts shirt, aching to play for the club he loves? I doubt it.

Currently, there are plans to move Hearts away from Tynecastle to Murrayfield. This is not a new suggestion – I can remember the idea being mooted as far back as the 1950s. Whilst I am emotionally bound to the ground, I recognise the need for change and therefore would not oppose such a move on the principle of my love for Tynecastle. Other clubs have successfully left their old spiritual homes and thrived in new, modern stadiums. Equally, though, I believe such a move should not be forced on the fans without serious consultation and a plan that proves that the ground move is the bedrock of a serious strategy to improve the fortunes of Heart of Midlothian FC and revive the glory days.

For me, the biggest threat to our game is the question of where the new players come from. Although I look for them, I cannot find the games of football being played in the parks and streets by the local kids. Many of the old playing fields are gone; they now boast luxury flats (are no 'ordinary' flats built any more?) and vast supermarkets have sprung up on the land where our jumpers once lay as goalposts. Even the backstreets are full of cars. When I was at Hearts and playing professionally, I still went over to the park on a Sunday and joined in the games, as did other young pros from Hibernian and other clubs, such was our hunger. I couldn't see that happening today.

Kids nowadays have too much choice. They've got their Sky TV; they've got their Gameboys, their DVDs and their Internet. It's no surprise that going over to the park and playing football might not be their first choice for passing the time. In my day, we had only one choice. Play football or sit indoors and watch Mum knitting. It wasn't difficult. The sedentary lifestyle adopted by children is a worry that goes far beyond football. To be physically fit is to be mentally fit. When I was young there was always one, maybe two, fat kids in the school, but look into a playground now (if you dare – watching kids play now being almost a hanging offence) and see the children waddling around. It's not nice. Find a country where the kids still play in the streets (and there are some) and you will find the World Cup winners of the future.

In addition to the pure physical decline in children, we also now live in a society where to win or want to win is almost a crime. One of my grandchildren told me they play rugby at school, but it is a version where no physical contact is allowed. Rugby without physical contact? How does that work?

Only recently, I picked up the *Sunday Times* and read the following article. I had to check it was not April Fool's Day. Sadly not, and this in my home town of Edinburgh:

> Football is facing a new pitch invasion by the politically correct. Officials plan to protect junior players from the trauma of losing by resetting the score to 0–0 at half-time and allowing the weaker team to field two extra players. Under new rules for school matches, children in Edinburgh will kick off next season safe in the knowledge

that if they are five goals behind at half-time, the score will be cancelled. The rules are being supported by the Scottish Football Association. A Football Association spokesman said: 'The idea fits into our ethos of focusing on junior players having fun and not putting emphasis on the result.'

If this is truly what it has come to, then what hope is there? These people and these attitudes are truly sealing the fate of the Scottish national team and condemning us as a footballing nation to permanent mediocrity.

We have become ashamed of our historical victories, too. How many schoolchildren today have the faintest idea who Admiral Nelson, Robert Bruce or the Duke of Wellington were? How long before Sir Geoff Hurst's name must be whispered and the image of Bobby Moore holding the World Cup aloft is banned, lest we upset the Germans? The great British athletes of the past succeeded because they possessed the spirit to win and the hunger to be the victor. It is a spirit that has been passed down the generations. In this climate, I cannot see that spirit surviving. Already, it is a struggle to persuade some players to find the time to represent their countries and we tolerate it.

I sometimes become depressed by all these threats to the game that I love. But then again, I am hopelessly nostalgic. Young people have their lives to look forward to, older people have their lives to look back on. Am I the only man in Britain who misses the sound of a whistling kettle? But maybe I'm wrong and everything in the garden is rosy, my perspective disproportionately skewed by my connection to the past.

Yet there are times when everything is fine and I feel, momentarily, positively blissful. It normally happens in bed just as dawn is breaking. It is those few moments just between sleeping and waking, and the dream you have been having is still real. People normally use the expression 'it was like a dream' to indicate some hazy, out of body, almost supernatural experience. But the point is, for me, that dreams are real. When they are happening and immediately afterwards, as far as your mind is concerned, that *is* happening or *has* happened. There is no sense of it being a dream. That is why they can be so uplifting: it is only here you can be with friends and relatives again that are certainly not around when you are awake, and that is why nightmares can be so terrifying. That is why this dream, when I remember it in those minutes before the alarm clock goes off and the house is quiet, is so special.

I'm in the middle of a big game down on the fields near Glendevon Park. All my brothers are there. Mum and Dad are standing around watching. A boy scores and turns around, grinning. It's John White. His hair is blowing in the wind. Johnny Haynes slide-tackles me and brown mud splatters us both. We start laughing. Everyone is out there playing together: Willie Bauld, Jimmy Wardhaugh, Alfie Conn, Eric Smith, Ralph Brand, Danny Blanchflower, Jimmy Greaves, Bobby Smith, Cliff Jones, Denis Law, Ron Henry, Maurice Norman, Jim Baxter, Roy McFarland, John Robson, Kevin Hector, Charlie George and scores of others. Boys who really were on that field with me 60 years ago and who I have not seen since are interspersed with the likes of George Best and Eusebio and men 30 years younger than themselves. Like all dreams, it makes no sense. Players whom I never knew personally and I have never given a thought to in four decades make appearances. Every one of them is frozen in time as a boy – some of those people I did not know as boys, but I am positive that is how they were when they were younger. There is no story. There is no beginning and there is no end. A few blinks of the eye and everyone has receded. I'm already struggling to capture the detail. I turn my head and Isobel is asleep next to me. Life was good. Life is good.

Epilogue

I travel back to Edinburgh once or twice every year. There remain many family and friends around to catch up with. I particularly enjoy attending the annual dinner at Hearts in memory of Willie Bauld. King Willie – the King of Hearts. I hope when my generation finally peters out that he will not be forgotten. He inspired so many. I also love my day out at Musselburgh races near Isobel's birthplace. I go most years and always meet up with old faces. Each time I bump into a man named Ronald Macdonald (he had the name first) and we bemoan our complete failure to back a decent horse and the inexorable march of time. Ronald used to watch me at Hearts and has said some very kind things. This year we shook hands warmly and Ronald, who is now confined to a wheelchair, passed me an envelope. He asked me to read it later. I did and it brought a tear to the eye and smile to the lips. It read:

OCH AYE, DAVE MACKAY

When I think aboot the auld days,
What went oan in Edinburgh toon,
Hearts gawn through a bad phase,
And looked like going doon.
God couldnae let that happen,
Or watch auld reekie cry,
On speaking to his angels,
He sent Hearts Dave Mackay.

This bonnie lad frae Carricknowe,
So polite and so cool,
And footba he could play and how,
This kid was no one's fool.
Tynecastle never seen his like,
So dapper and so clever,
Gorgie Road, see the Jambos hike,
The queue went oan forever.

North, south, east or west,
Hearts put teams in their places,
By showing Jambos were the best,
Football flowing from their laces.
Who's playing for Hearts today?
You hear the Jambos cry,
Just the usual team,
And och aye Dave Mackay.

The finest player to touch a ba',
Handsome, strong and lean.
Cups and leagues, he won them aw,
It's no fair, says the Queen.
They transferred Dave to Tottenham
By royal intervention,
True enough this Scottish Ram,
Showed the English his intentions.

League, cups, Spurs won them aw,
Dave brought them great success.
When thinking that they had enough,
They put oot Dave tae grass.
Now Davey's gawn full circle,
Been tae Saudi and other places,
The only place he's never won,
Is at the Musselburgh Races.

Roll of Honour

PLAYING RECORD

Hearts, 1953–59
  played 184 games
  scored 34 goals

Tottenham Hotspur, 1959–68
  played 318 games
  scored 51 goals

Derby County, 1968–71
  played 145 games
  scored 7 goals

Swindon Town, 1971–72
  played 26 games
  scored 1 goal

MANAGERIAL RECORD

Swindon Town	1971–72	60 per cent of games undefeated
Nottingham Forest	1972–73	60 per cent of games undefeated
Derby County	1973–76	72 per cent of games undefeated

Walsall	1977–78	79 per cent of games undefeated
Al-Arabi, Kuwait	1978–86	90 per cent of games undefeated
Shabab Club, Dubai	1986–87	82 per cent of games undefeated
Doncaster Rovers	1987–89	46 per cent of games undefeated
Birmingham City	1989–91	66 per cent of games undefeated
Zamalek, Egypt	1991–93	86 per cent games of undefeated
Youth Team, Qatar	1993–96	Qualified for Under-17 World Cup, 1995

HONOURS

Scottish League Cup-winner's medal, Hearts – 1955, 1959

Scottish Cup-winner's medal, Hearts – 1956

Scottish League Championship medal, Hearts – 1958

Player of the Year award (*Sunday Mail*, 'Rex on Sunday') – 1959

English League Championship medal, Tottenham Hotspur – 1961

FA Cup-winner's medal, Tottenham Hotspur – 1961, 1962, 1967

English Second Division Championship medal, Derby County – 1969

FWA Footballer of the Year – 1969

English League Championship medal (as manager), Derby County – 1975

Various championships, cups, the Double and Treble in Kuwait (Al Arabi), Dubai (Shabab Club), Egypt (Zamalek) and Qatar (youth international side) – 1978–96

22 caps for Scotland –1957–66

CAPTAIN

Hearts

Tottenham Hotspur

Derby County

Swindon Town

Scotland

Index